CW01665720

Prayers *for* Public Worship

Lent to Easter

David Adam
Nick Fawcett
Susan Sayers
Ray Simpson

kevin mayhew

kevin mayhew

First published in Great Britain in 2012 by Kevin Mayhew Ltd
Buxhall, Stowmarket, Suffolk IP14 3BW
Tel: +44 (0) 1449 737978 Fax: +44 (0) 1449 737834
E-mail: info@kevinmayhewltd.com

www.kevinmayhew.com

ISBN 978 1 84867 573 5
Catalogue No. 1501388

Cover design by Rob Mortonson

Typeset by Richard Weaver

Printed and bound in Great Britain

Contents

	Prayer nos.
Lent	1–131
Mothering Sunday	132–153
Palm Sunday	154–181
Holy Week	182–197
Maundy Thursday	198–209
Good Friday	210–234
Saturday (Easter Eve)	235–240
Easter	241–325

About the authors

DAVID ADAM was the Vicar of Lindisfarne, off the Northumbrian coast, for thirteen years until he retired in March 2003. His work involved ministering to thousands of pilgrims and other visitors. He is the author of many inspiring books on spirituality and prayer, and his Celtic writings have rekindled a keen interest in our Christian heritage.

NICK FAWCETT was brought up in Southend-on-Sea, Essex, and trained for the Baptist ministry at Bristol and Oxford, before serving churches in Lancashire and Cheltenham. He subsequently spent three years as a chaplain with the Christian movement Toc H, before focusing on writing and editing, which he continues with today, despite wrestling with cancer. He lives with his wife, Deborah, and two children – Samuel and Kate – in Wellington, Somerset, worshipping at the local Anglican church. A keen walker, he delights in the beauty of the Somerset and Devon countryside around his home, his numerous books owing much to the inspiration he unfailingly finds there.

SUSAN SAYERS is the author of many popular resource books for the church. Through the conferences and workshops she is invited to lead, she has been privileged to share in the worship of many different traditions and cultures. A teacher by profession, she was ordained a priest in the Anglican Church and, before her retirement, her work was divided between the parish of Westcliff-on-Sea, the local women's prison, writing, training days and retreats.

RAY SIMPSON is a Celtic new monastic for tomorrow's world, a lecturer, consultant, liturgist, and author of some 30 books. He is the founding guardian of the international Community of Aidan and Hilda and the pioneer of its e-studies programmes. He is an ordained member of the Christian church and lives on the Holy Island of Lindisfarne. His website is www.raysimpson.org

Lent

1 God,
we thank you for your redeeming love.
You have sent your Son to be our Saviour.
You have rescued us from darkness and death
and given us eternal life.
To you, Lord, be praise and glory for ever. *David Adam*

2 Lord God,
we thank you
for the coming of Christ into the world
and sharing in our troubles.
We rejoice in your saving power
and in the promise of life eternal.
We pray for all who seek to walk the way of the cross.
We remember pilgrims in Jerusalem
and we ask your blessing
upon all Christians who are facing persecution
and rejection at this time. *David Adam*

3 Lord Jesus,
who walked the way of the cross
and gave yourself willingly for us,
help us to be generous in our living
and to give ourselves to you. *David Adam*

4 Remind us, Lord,
of the true cost of living,
and your willingness, through your Son,
to pay it.
Help us to receive and celebrate the life made possible
through him –
life in all its fullness –
and to give something back in return to you
who gave so much. *Nick Fawcett*

5 Lord Jesus Christ,
you faced temptation in the wilderness –
enticement to put yourself first,
to seek worldly glory,
to compromise your calling –

and steadfastly you refused.
You faced pressure throughout your ministry –
hostility,
ridicule,
threats,
rejection –
yet you carried on regardless,
true to your message,
true to your mission.
You faced the greatest test of all in Gethsemane,
as you wrestled there
with the prospect of betrayal, denial, suffering and death,
but once again you held firm,
putting God's will before your own.
What you said and what you did were always one,
each testifying to the other.
Lord Jesus Christ,
we fall so short of that goal,
words coming easily,
deeds to match rarely coming at all.
Forgive us,
and help us to show in our lives
the things we proclaim with our lips,
to your praise and glory. *Nick Fawcett*

6 Living God,
it's easy to fool ourselves that we are observing Lent –
giving up certain vices,
denying ourselves particular pleasures,
and making fine-sounding resolutions –
but deep down we know that Lent should be more than this:
a time rather for prayer and reflection,
for self-examination and renewed commitment.
We come, then, seeking your will,
your word,
your guidance
and your grace.
Nurture our feeble faith
and help us to put you at the centre of this season,

so that through it we may know you better,
love you more fully
and serve you more effectively,
to the glory of your name. *Nick Fawcett*

7 Search us, O God, and know our thoughts.
Examine us and reveal our faults.
Cleanse us and make us new.
Touch us and make us whole.
Equip us and give us strength.
Meet us and speak your word.
Hear us and accept our worship,
in Jesus' name. *Nick Fawcett*

8 Redeemer God,
we come in this season of Lent,
conscious of our weakness,
dismayed by the feebleness of our faith,
and yearning to show penitence
at our inability to serve you as we would and should.
But we come also gladly
and with confidence,
knowing that you are a gracious God,
slow to punish and swift to forgive,
always looking to bless, restore and renew.
Remind us of that truth as we worship you,
both now and in the days ahead,
so that true repentance may be matched by true thanksgiving,
and sorrow at our many faults be balanced
by rejoicing at your inestimable love and mercy.
In Christ's name we pray. *Nick Fawcett*

9 Living God,
we would offer this day in worship,
but we are so easily led astray,
our minds preoccupied with other concerns,
our attention caught by trivia,
our sense of expectation eroded by familiarity.

We would offer our lives in service,
but it is a similar story,
our faith so often suffocated by the cares of each day,
our discipleship put second to what can never truly satisfy,
our relationship with you taken for granted
and allowed to stagnate.
Through this time together,
and this season,
call us back to you.
Remind us of essentials,
challenge us concerning our priorities
and restore us to your side,
so that when temptation comes
we will stay as true to you as you are true to us.

Nick Fawcett

10 Lord Jesus Christ,
prepare your way in our hearts
and make us ready to worship you.
Through our praying, thinking, singing and reading
cleanse our thoughts,
kindle our faith,
renew our commitment
and increase our love,
preparing your way in our lives,
so that we might be ready to follow you faithfully
and serve you more effectively,
to the glory of your name.

Nick Fawcett

11 Redeemer Christ,
we come to acknowledge you again as our Lord and Saviour;
to declare our faith in you as the one who sets us free,
delivering us from all that holds us captive
and denies us life.
Yet we come also knowing how easily we turn serving you
into serving self,
being happy enough to receive
but reluctant to give,

ready to profess allegiance when it suits us
but unwilling to take up our cross should following
prove costly.
Equip us, then, through our worship,
to honour you not just with protestations of loyalty
but above all with lives committed to your kingdom
and lived in obedience to your will.
In your name we pray. *Nick Fawcett*

12 Lord Jesus Christ,
speak to us of the new life you have made possible
through your stupendous sacrifice,
your willingness to surrender all.
Unfold to us the true nature of discipleship –
what it means to love and follow you –
and help us, by your grace, to respond,
dying to self and rising to new life with you,
so that all we do and are may be by your power,
in your service
and to your glory. *Nick Fawcett*

13 Sovereign God,
we would draw close and learn of you,
so that we might know, love and serve you better.
Receive, then, the worship we bring
and meet us through it,
speaking your word,
offering your guidance,
imparting your strength
and granting your mercy.
Give us a clearer understanding of your will
and help us to recognise everything in our lives
that conspires against it;
that leads us astray,
separating us from you and one another.
Grant us grace to resist temptation,
and to walk in your way,
now and always. *Nick Fawcett*

14 Sovereign God,
as Peter, James and John caught a glimpse of your radiance
on the mountaintop,
revealed in Christ,
so may we today see your glory more clearly –
your light shining in our hearts,
firing our imagination,
filling us with joy
and fanning the flames of faith.
Help us, confronted by the mystery and wonder of
your presence,
to recognise that, however much we have understood,
you have far more to reveal,
our grasp of your greatness and experience of your love
still partial,
needing always to be open to new horizons.
Speak, then, and open our eyes,
in the name of Christ. *Nick Fawcett*

15 Lord Jesus Christ,
we praise you for your ministry,
your love,
your faithfulness to your calling.
We thank you for your willingness to face even death itself
so that we might find the true meaning of life.
We thank you for that sense of purpose,
that inner courage,
that deep faith which gave you the strength
to continue on your chosen path
to the very end.
Lord Jesus Christ,
forgive us that having received so much we give so little
in return.
Forgive us that we shy away from sacrifice and self-denial.
Forgive us for taking the easy and less costly way
rather than the way of the cross.
Help us to deny ourselves
and so to find life in all its fullness.
In your name we ask it. *Nick Fawcett*

16 Lord Jesus Christ, 2/4/17
no one can ever give us more than you have given,
for you have blessed us with life itself –
life overflowing with good things,
life eternal –
and to make that gift possible you gave of yourself,
not just a little but all.
You bore the limitations of human flesh;
you endured rejection,
humiliation and, finally, death on a cross;
and, most awesome of all,
you took on yourself the dreadful burden of this world's sinfulness,
experiencing despair and isolation for our sakes.
Forgive us that, despite all this,
we give so grudgingly in return.
Forgive us that though our words say one thing
our lives say another;
that our thoughts are so little for you
and still less for others.
Help us to catch again a glimpse of the love you have so freely given
and so may we spontaneously give of ourselves
in joyful and heartfelt thanksgiving,
for your name's sake. *Nick Fawcett*

17 Examine us, Lord,
and know our thoughts.
Search us,
and help us to see where we are spiritually weak,
our faith lacking and our commitment poor.
Put a new heart and a right spirit within us,
and, by your grace,
make us whole. *Nick Fawcett*

18 You call us to imitate you, Lord –
to reflect something of your light and love in our lives,
but we find it so hard,
the picture we give to others
proving a feeble caricature of who and what you are.

Though we will always fall short,
help us, we pray,
to be a little more like Jesus,
our lives in some way speaking to others of him.

Nick Fawcett

19 Lord,
we talk glibly of sacrifice and self-denial,
when in reality we live almost wholly for our own ends,
unwilling to surrender even a little for you or others.
We daily deny you.
Give us a genuine commitment to Christ that shows itself in action;
a faith that makes a difference to who and what we are,
unmistakable to all. *Nick Fawcett*

20 Examine us, Lord,
and show us what's wrong in our lives.
Search us,
and help us to recognise where we go astray.
Teach us to look carefully at who and what we are,
identifying our faults and weaknesses,
and, with your help,
seeking to put them right,
so that, imperfect though we are,
we may approximate more nearly
to what we're meant to be
and what we hunger to become. *Nick Fawcett*

21 Help us to see, Lord,
where our relationship with you is not as it should be,
not as secure or as close as we like to think.
However trivial our faults may seem,
save us from taking them too lightly –
from putting off tackling them so long
that things slip once too often
and we fall completely from your side. *Nick Fawcett*

22 Forgive us, Lord,
for we're careless in discipleship,
reluctant to move away from the comfort zone.
Forgive the complacency of our commitment,
our doing as little rather than as much as possible,
and teach us to offer instead not what we must
but what we may do in your service,
in glad and joyful response. *Nick Fawcett*

23 Though we don't mean to be proud, Lord,
we can't resist sometimes the odd sense of smugness,
the temptation to belittle others
and think of ourselves more highly than we should.
Forgive us, and help us to follow the pattern of Christ,
remembering that he,
though greater than all,
counted himself as nothing,
emptying himself to the point of death
in order to raise us to life.
Teach us, then,
to count others better than ourselves,
looking to their interests before our own. *Nick Fawcett*

24 Forgive us, Lord,
for we spend so long yearning for what we haven't got
instead of celebrating what we have.
Teach us to appreciate our many blessings
and not to begrudge others theirs. *Nick Fawcett*

25 Teach us, Lord,
to confess our sins to you
instead of struggling with guilt or hiding away in fear;
to let go of the burden,
knowing that you seek to pardon rather than condemn,
bless instead of punish.
Help us, then,
openly and honestly to acknowledge our faults,
so that we may find the freedom you alone can give.
Nick Fawcett

26 Forgive us, Lord,
for, time after time,
we put you on hold,
making time for you when it suits us
but then turning to other things,
forgetting you are even there.
Whatever we're doing,
wherever we are,
help us stay connected –
ready to listen to your voice and to respond. *Nick Fawcett*

27 Forgive us, Lord,
for too easily we forget you,
repeatedly overlooking your presence,
and failing, sometimes for days on end,
even to give you a second thought.
Teach us what matters most in life –
your love, your will,
your grace, your goodness –
and whatever else we may forget,
may we remember you. *Nick Fawcett*

28 Lord God,
all good, all pure, all holy,
forgive us the many ways we fail you
and our own responsibility in that failure.
Teach us to shun temptation,
avoiding as best we can whatever may cause us to stumble,
and so may we walk,
this day and always,
in newness of life.
In Christ's name we ask it. *Nick Fawcett*

29 Living God,
cleanse us from within
and purge us of everything that keeps us from you.
Nick Fawcett

30 Sovereign God,
for the many ways we fail to live as your people,
forgive us.
Guard us from temptation
and teach us to live by your Spirit. *Nick Fawcett*

31 Living God,
forgive us that, too easily, we slip into a faith of negatives,
imagining that you are more concerned with what we shouldn't do
than with what we should.
Teach us that, although there is a very real place for self-denial,
there is also a place for affirming and celebrating life in all its fullness.
Help us, then, to use this season of Lent as a time to grow and learn,
to deepen our faith and strengthen our commitment;
above all,
as a time to make more room for you,
so that you can work in our lives
and enrich our experience of your love,
through Jesus Christ our Lord. *Nick Fawcett*

32 Loving God,
you tell us that we will not be tested beyond our limits,
that we shall not be tempted beyond what we can withstand.
But you tell us also to examine ourselves,
to consider our faith,
ensuring that we are serving and honouring you as we should be.
Forgive us that we all too easily grow casual in our discipleship,
dismissing the need for such soul-searching.
Forgive us that we are content to meander along the way of discipleship,
rather than dedicate ourselves single-mindedly to your service.
Help us to learn from the example of Jesus,
and to remember that even he experienced a time of testing,
and even he had to wrestle with temptation.

Give us grace, then, to be honest with ourselves
and honest with you,
so that we may stand firm in faith
whatever temptations we might face.
In Christ's name we ask it. *Nick Fawcett*

33 Eternal God,
as we worship you today and throughout this season of Lent,
help us to recognise all that is wrong in our lives,
all that separates us from you and others,
all that obstructs your purpose,
leads us into temptation
and causes us to fall.
Help us, prayerfully and humbly, to examine ourselves
and honestly acknowledge our faults,
not so that we might wallow in self-pity or indulge in false piety,
but so that we may receive cleansing, healing and forgiveness –
renewal in body, mind and spirit,
through Jesus Christ our Lord. *Nick Fawcett*

34 Lord Jesus Christ,
we mean to be faithful to you,
to live as you have called us to,
but somehow we repeatedly end up
turning the positive message of the gospel
into a list of negatives,
a matter of rules and regulations rather than grateful response,
a law that imprisons rather than a love that liberates.
Forgive us,
and teach us again your way –
the way of mercy and understanding that leads to life.
In your name we pray. *Nick Fawcett*

35 Lord Jesus Christ,
faced with difficult decisions
so often we tell ourselves we have no choice,
that life has pushed us into a corner,
leaving us no alternative as to how to act.

But in our hearts we know that isn't so.
It may be hard, painful or costly,
but finally there is always a right way
if we are prepared to look for it.
Forgive us for all the excuses we make.
Forgive us for the ways we wriggle and squirm
rather than face up to our responsibilities.
Forgive us for all the times we have taken the soft option
rather than the one we know to be right.
Teach us, next time we have to make a choice,
to seek your will,
to listen to your voice
and to respond in faith,
to the glory of your name. *Nick Fawcett*

36 Gracious God,
forgive us our mean and selfish spirit –
our desire so often to safeguard pleasures for ourselves,
to provide for our own well-being while ignoring the needs of others.
Teach us that it is in giving we receive,
in denying ourselves that we discover true riches.
Help us not just to assent to that truth intellectually,
but also to believe it in our hearts and show it in our lives.
Give us a heart overflowing with generosity,
eager to share with others the good things you have given us,
and in so doing may we add to their joy and our own,
through Jesus Christ our Lord. *Nick Fawcett*

37 Lord Jesus Christ,
we want to follow your example
and we strive to do so,
but so often our weakness gets the better of us.
We talk of serving others
but live instead for ourselves;
we speak of self-sacrifice
but indulge our self-interest;
we profess loyalty to your cause,
yet repeatedly deny it through the way we live.

We have preferred our ways to yours,
more concerned with our own advancement than
your kingdom.
We have been weak in our commitment
and half-hearted in offering our service.
Forgive us all the ways our lives fail to reflect your goodness
and all the ways our faithlessness betrays your grace.
Touch our lives afresh
and fill our hearts with your love
so that we may truly live for you,
making known your love
and bringing closer your kingdom.
In your name we ask it. *Nick Fawcett*

38 Loving God,
you know us better than we know ourselves,
you search our hearts, minds and souls,
seeing us as we really are and confronting us with our
true selves.
Forgive us that all too often we shy away,
refusing to accept anything
that contradicts the image we have of ourselves.
Forgive us that we find it hard to be honest,
closing our ears to truths we would rather not hear.
Forgive us for preferring those who soothe and flatter
our egos
rather than those who challenge and disturb.
Give us true humility that we may be ready to
examine ourselves,
ready to ask searching questions,
and ready to change where necessary. *Nick Fawcett*

39 Too easily, Lord,
and at this season in particular,
we picture you with a frown on your face –
stern,
forbidding,
angry –
as though you are permanently displeased at our behaviour,
looking for the opportunity to step in and condemn.

Remind us that the reality is so very different,
your nature always to have mercy,
to forgive, love and accept.
Help us, then,
during Lent and always,
to celebrate your love that smiles upon us. *Nick Fawcett*

40 Thank you, Lord,
that you do not compel us to serve
but rather invite us to respond –
calling us to serve you of our own free will.
Give us the self-discipline we need to do that:
to hear your voice and respond,
honouring your will and playing our part
in the work of your kingdom.
Help us to fulfil our responsibilities to you,
as faithfully as we can. *Nick Fawcett*

41 Almighty and all-seeing God,
we thank you for this season of Lent:
a time to reflect upon our discipleship,
to consider our calling,
to examine ourselves
and to assess the health of our faith.
Help us to be honest in this:
to see ourselves as we really are
with all our weaknesses, ugliness and sinfulness.
Help us to face the things we usually prefer to push aside;
the unpleasant truths we sweep under the carpet,
pretending they are not there.
Help us to come to you now,
acknowledging our faults,
recognising our weaknesses
and receiving your forgiveness,
which alone can make us whole,
through the grace of Christ. *Nick Fawcett*

42 Gracious God,
we thank you for the astonishing love you showed in Christ,
sharing our humanity through him.
We praise you that you became flesh and blood like us,
experiencing the same temptations we face,
torn by the same fears,
suffering the same pain
and tasting the same joys and sorrows.
For the assurance this brings –
the knowledge that you understand the worries, concerns,
doubts and problems that confront us each day –
receive our worship,
in the name of Christ.

Nick Fawcett

43 Gracious God,
we thank you for the time spent by Jesus in the wilderness,
tested there to the limit but refusing to be deceived.
Help us to learn from his example;
to be awake to temptation and ready to withstand it;
to make time to hear your voice
and reflect upon your word.
Help us to follow you and to do your will,
regardless of the cost.
So may we grow closer to you and stronger in our faith.

Nick Fawcett

44 We remember, Lord God,
how Jesus had to choose in the wilderness
between the way of self or others –
and how he chose the latter,
knowing it would mean suffering and sacrifice,
the agony of death on a cross,
and that once he started out
there could be no turning back.
Help us to follow you with similar commitment,
ready to walk your way to our journey's end.

Nick Fawcett

45 Remind us, Lord,
that we need to pause sometimes if we're to make sense of life;
to stop and stare if we're to keep things in balance
and live as you intend.
In the many demands and duties we face each day,
teach us to make time for stillness and quiet –
to find space for ourselves and for you. *Nick Fawcett*

46 Too often, Lord,
the flame of our faith dies down,
the commitment that once burned so brightly
left barely smouldering,
our enthusiasm turned cold.
Yet, from the dying embers,
you bring new life,
rekindling the fire of faith.
Come now,
and reignite our love,
so that it may burn afresh for you. *Nick Fawcett*

47 Teach us, Lord,
that your call to seek and find is not a one-off instruction –
advice we can act on once and then forget about –
but an indispensable guideline for discipleship,
to be persevered with throughout the journey of faith.
Help us, then,
to search patiently for greater understanding
and deeper commitment –
a fuller love for you and others –
assured that if we truly seek such things,
we will find. *Nick Fawcett*

48 Teach us, Lord,
that, however strong our faith or deep our commitment,
if love is missing then the rest is flawed,
and all the devotion and piety in the world
can never redress the balance.

Whatever else we lack, then,
may your love flow within us –
the ground and goal of all our being. *Nick Fawcett*

49 Help us, Lord,
for our happiness is so easily undermined,
so many of the goals we strive for offering illusory satisfaction,
here today and gone tomorrow.
Teach us to build wisely,
seeking fulfilment in your love,
which, alone, is able to face the restless tide
and still stand firm,
for ever. *Nick Fawcett*

50 Remind us, Lord,
that nothing in this life lasts for ever;
the world's beauty, joy and pleasure,
special though they are,
being all too fleeting,
ours but for a moment.
Help us, then,
to celebrate such gifts,
but never to pin our happiness upon them;
to seek instead treasure in heaven
that will neither fade nor perish. *Nick Fawcett*

51 You offer in Christ, Lord,
a picture of what life can be,
what we can be –
everything made new –
yet we struggle to believe it possible,
for we fall so far short
and find it hard to change even a little.
Teach us that,
provided we're serious about commitment
and prepared to play our part,
you can do what we can't,
from the unpromising material of our lives
fashioning a new creation. *Nick Fawcett*

52 Remind us, Lord,
that the journey of discipleship isn't over,
however far we may have come;
that each day brings new roads and horizons to explore,
so much still lying before us.
Save us in this life from ever thinking we've arrived,
but, instead, keep us travelling with you,
until the pilgrimage is over,
and we enter your kingdom at last. *Nick Fawcett*

53 Teach us, Lord,
to use this season to set new targets,
more ambitious goals,
resolving to know, love and serve you better.
Though we've failed before and will fail again,
instead of being content merely to plod along
may we truly strive to grow in grace. *Nick Fawcett*

54 May your love, Lord,
keep hold of us in the daily round of life.
Though we're buffeted by temptation
and exposed to the wind of change,
save us from being tossed about by the restless current.
Secure us through your love
so that we shall not go astray. *Nick Fawcett*

55 Help us to give something up for Lent, Lord,
not because it's expected or out of empty show
but to promote our spiritual health.
Enable us, with your help,
to cut out whatever undermines our discipleship,
denying your love and frustrating your purpose;
whatever, in other words,
creates a barrier between us,
preventing us from knowing you
as we should and could. *Nick Fawcett*

56 Help us, Lord,
to respect your gifts and treat them wisely,
conscious that they may be a blessing or a curse,
a treasure or a toxin.
Help us to celebrate the good things you offer,
and to use rather than abuse them. *Nick Fawcett*

57 We try not to be selfish, Lord –
mean and grudging in our giving –
but too often we're not as generous as we should be,
more concerned to hold on to our money than to share it.
Teach us to steward our resources wisely
but equally to give of them freely,
lest what we possess ends up possessing us. *Nick Fawcett*

58 Are we doing enough, Lord –
as much as we like to think –
or do we make excuses,
putting off what we'd rather not face?
Help us truly to serve you,
not doing as little as we can get away with
but going the extra mile,
giving and giving again
to you who gave your all for us. *Nick Fawcett*

59 Almighty God,
teach us what it means to love,
what it takes to follow you,
what it costs to serve you,
and help us to stay true when testing comes,
choosing your way and walking it faithfully
with all our heart and mind and soul. *Nick Fawcett*

60 Living God,
create in us a thirst to know you better,
a hunger to grow in grace
and a yearning to mature in discipleship.
Prompt, guide and instruct through your Spirit,
and so deepen our faith a little more each day,
to your praise and glory. *Nick Fawcett*

61 Living God,
in Christ you have showed us a new way,
an approach to life and to others different to that of the world.
Teach us what it means to follow that path,
and help us to walk it faithfully,
by the grace of Christ. *Nick Fawcett*

62 Living God,
save us from being led astray
by those who proclaim what we want to hear,
teach what we want to believe,
urge what we want to follow,
and propound what we find easy to accept.
Open our ears to voices that challenge and disturb,
trouble and unsettle,
question and confront.
Open our ears to all who speak in your name. *Nick Fawcett*

63 Living God,
show us the path we must tread,
guide our footsteps,
and keep us from going astray.
However hard the way,
help us to continue faithfully along it,
walking with perseverance
until we reach our journey's end. *Nick Fawcett*

64 Lord Jesus Christ,
help us,
through honouring your commandment to love,
to honour all the commandments,
testifying to the truth of the law and the prophets in word and deed,
and giving daily expression to the fulfilment these have found in you. *Nick Fawcett*

65 Loving God,
awaken in us a hunger to know you better,
a yearning to grow in faith
and a longing to serve you more faithfully.
Show us our need and the way you alone can meet it,
through Christ our Lord. *Nick Fawcett*

66 Loving God,
grant that all the blessings we have,
the good things that surround us,
may never cause us to overlook the treasure
you have given us in Christ,
the riches of life in abundance, eternal and ever-new.
Nick Fawcett

67 Sovereign God,
give us strength to love you,
serve you and stand firm for you,
even when faith involves sacrifice
and commitment entails cost. *Nick Fawcett*

68 Sovereign God,
when discipleship involves confronting evil
and commitment means standing up to be counted,
grant us courage to stay true to you and to accept the cost,
through Jesus Christ our Lord. *Nick Fawcett*

69 Lord Jesus Christ,
teach us when to say 'yes' and when to say 'no',
and help us not only to take those decisions
but also to stick to them once taken. *Nick Fawcett*

70 Gracious God,
teach us to wrestle with our sin,
our doubts,
our fears and our weaknesses,
and, in battling with those,
may we find we have taken hold of you,
through Christ our Lord. *Nick Fawcett*

71 Loving God,
teach us to see beneath the surface
and to recognise that good and evil bring their own reward.
So may we live with integrity,
intent on doing your will. *Nick Fawcett*

72 Gracious God,
despite our resolve to serve you we are so easily led astray.
Like sheep,
we blindly follow the example of the crowd.
We congratulate ourselves on resisting the latest trend
or fashion,
but the pressures to conform are more subtle than that,
often unseen,
unrecognised.
Help us to listen to you rather than the voices that
surround us,
to stay close to your side and respond to your guidance.
And, should we find ourselves lost,
seek us out through Christ, the Good Shepherd,
and restore us to your fold,
for his name's sake. *Nick Fawcett*

73 Lord Jesus Christ,
sometimes you present us with a choice:
between right and wrong,
good and evil,
life and death.
We know the way we ought to take,
but we know also the cost,
so we hold back,
passing the buck instead to others.
Yet eventually we cannot evade your challenge,
for in the very act of avoiding we make our decision.
Lord Jesus Christ,
give us courage to face the choices life brings,
and give us wisdom to choose the right way. *Nick Fawcett*

74 Lord Jesus Christ,
as you wrestled in the wilderness with temptation,
with the nature of your calling
and your ability to meet what it would cost you,
so help us today
and throughout this time of Lent
to hear your voice,
to understand what you ask of us
and to consider our response.
Fasten our thoughts on you,
and direct all that we do,
so that we might grow in grace
and stand firm in faith,
able to resist whatever might cause us to fall.
In your name we pray. *Nick Fawcett*

75 God of all,
conscious of our weakness but trusting in your grace
we come now before you,
consecrating this service,
this day
and this season to you.
Grant that today,
and this time of Lent,
may draw us closer to you,
so that, acknowledging the frailty of our faith
and limitations of our discipleship,
we might find pardon and cleansing,
guidance and inspiration,
strength and blessing,
equipping us to walk more faithfully in the days ahead,
through Jesus Christ our Lord. *Nick Fawcett*

76 Lord Jesus Christ,
just as you walked and talked on our earth,
present among your people,
sharing our humanity,
ministering your love,
living and dying alongside us,
teach us that you are here now through your Spirit,

equally as near and involved,
just as eager to show your love and minister your grace.
Grant, as we come together in your name,
that we might sense your presence,
hear your voice
and learn more of your redeeming, renewing power,
so that we will be open to all you would do among us
and equipped to live more faithfully as your people,
seeking your kingdom. *Nick Fawcett*

77 Lord Jesus Christ,
again we ask you to teach us more of your way –
to open our hearts and minds to your presence among us
and to your work in our lives and our world.
Help us, today, to understand more clearly
the nature of your kingdom,
growing inexorably among us despite all that frustrates your will
and conspires against your love.
Equip us simply but sincerely to respond to you,
committing ourselves wholeheartedly to discipleship
and doing whatever we can in our own small way
to bring your kingdom closer,
here on earth as it is in heaven. *Nick Fawcett*

78 Gracious God,
we forget sometimes that alongside the blessings of discipleship
there is always the cost –
sacrifices that will be asked of us;
demands upon our time, energy, gifts and money;
responsibilities we must accept.
Help us to respond gladly to your call,
knowing that, however great the price may be,
the rewards are infinitely worth it.
Teach us to offer whatever you ask,
looking to that day when we rejoice in everything you hold in store
for all your people,
through Jesus Christ our Lord. *Nick Fawcett*

79 Living God,
it is uncomfortable sometimes having to choose.
We prefer to sit on the fence,
to hedge our bets,
to take the path of compromise in the hope of pleasing all.
Even when we know the right way,
we turn aside from it,
fearful of the cost that may be involved.
Yet, deep down, we know this simply won't do;
that failing to decide for you means deciding against you.
Help us to recognise when we need to make a choice,
and then give us courage to stand firm in faith,
whatever it may cost. *Nick Fawcett*

80 Lord Jesus Christ,
it is easy to talk of taking up our cross and following you,
but the reality is different.
We find it hard to deny ourselves even a little,
let alone to give our all.
There is so much we want to enjoy,
so much we want to achieve,
and the thought of sacrificing any of that
is one we would rather push aside.
Yet you have taught that it is in losing our lives we truly find them,
and that we shall find lasting treasure not on earth but in heaven.
Help us, then, instead of clinging slavishly to self-interest,
to give of ourselves freely,
just as you gave yourself for us. *Nick Fawcett*

81 Loving God,
we think we are so busy, so pressurised, having so much to do.
We rush around day after day with never a moment to spare.
Yet so often we forget the one thing we really need –
to make time and space in our lives to meet with you,
to hear your voice,
and to look at the world from your perspective.
Loving God, teach us to be still and know your presence.
Nick Fawcett

82 Help us to make a difference, Lord –
if not to be salt of the earth
then at least to change something,
somewhere,
for the better.
Help us,
through serving others,
to serve you. *Nick Fawcett*

83 Lord Jesus,
throughout your life you were the man for others,
always ready to listen,
always prepared to respond,
whatever the cost to yourself.
At your death it was the same –
still you poured yourself out,
thinking of others to the last.
Forgive us that we are the opposite,
more often than not our thoughts only for self,
rarely willing to listen,
even less so to respond,
fearful of what it all might cost us.
Throughout our lives we are the same,
reluctant to give of ourselves,
thinking of our own interests to the last.
We do not mean to do it,
but it is the way we are,
hard though we try to be different.
Lord Jesus,
forgive us and teach us your way,
for until we learn to be the servant of all
we will continue to be the slave of self.
Help us to give freely,
and in a life of service to find true freedom. *Nick Fawcett*

84 Living God,
you challenge us to go the extra mile,
to do more than anyone can ask or expect of us.

Forgive us that we find that so hard:
that we prefer to do as little as possible rather than as much;
that we give our help, time, service and money
grudgingly rather than cheerfully.
We praise you for the readiness of Christ to go not just the extra mile
but to give his all,
identifying himself with our human condition,
willingly experiencing suffering and death
so that we might discover life in its fullness.
We praise you for those who have followed in his footsteps,
willing to go beyond the call of duty in the service of others.
Touch our hearts through their example
and inspire us through the love of Christ,
so that we may be more ready to do that little bit extra,
to go beyond people's expectations,
to give as you have given to us so freely.
In the name of Christ we ask it. *Nick Fawcett*

85 Lord Jesus Christ,
we want to serve you,
and we like to believe we do,
but unwittingly we can turn even our faith
into a way of serving ourselves.
We gain strength through fellowship and worship,
but neglect your call to mission.
We focus on our own concerns in prayer
and forget about the world beyond.
Even our deeds of kindness
can finally be more about our own sense of righteousness
than the needs of those we think we are serving.
Lord Jesus,
help us to overcome the stranglehold of self
and to understand that true discipleship
brings its own reward,
for the more we give the more we shall receive.
In your mercy,
hear our prayer. *Nick Fawcett*

86 Lord Jesus Christ,
we are good at talking about service
but not very good at showing it.
We speak of your love for the helpless and hopeless,
but we all too rarely translate concern into action.
Forgive us the way we have neglected opportunities
to help others,
through deeds large or small.
Forgive the selfishness that has obscured love,
the greed that has denied compassion
and the laziness of body, mind and spirit
that has so often prevented any meaningful response.
Show us where and how we can serve in your name,
and inspire us to reach out in love,
offering something of ourselves to others,
even as you offered your all for us.
By your grace we ask it. *Nick Fawcett*

87 Lord Jesus Christ,
we proclaim you as our Lord and Saviour,
we believe you to be God's promised Messiah,
we preach the Gospel of your cross and resurrection.
Yet how often do we really listen to your message –
your message that challenges and disturbs,
that calls us to a life of self-denial and sacrifice,
that speaks of justice for the poor,
liberty for the imprisoned,
hope for the oppressed.
Lord Jesus, help us to hear not simply what we want to hear,
but rather what you would say to us. *Nick Fawcett*

88 Lord Jesus Christ,
we claim to be your followers working for your kingdom,
yet all too often we are reluctant
to get involved in the needs of our world.
We talk of service but are reluctant to roll our sleeves up.
We speak of compassion but keep the needy at arm's length.
Teach us not merely to talk of faith or speak of love,
but to show it. *Nick Fawcett*

89 As we begin this season of Lent
we ask you to remind us of what is important
and what is not;
of where we are wandering away
and what we need to change;
so that by Easter
we will be renewed and strengthened
for your service in the world. *Susan Sayers*

90 Jesus, you want us to be loving each day
and we say, 'OK!'
Jesus, you want us to do as you say
and we say, 'OK!' *Susan Sayers*

91 Lord Jesus,
when I am tempted to do what is wrong
and unloving and selfish,
make me brave
and keep me strong. *Susan Sayers*

92 As we call to mind the guidance and help
you give us each moment of every day,
we thank you and praise you, Holy God,
for you alone have the words of eternal life. *Susan Sayers*

93 Lord,
we give you thanks and praise
for the hope we have in Jesus;
for the strength to resist temptation
and the joy and relief of forgiveness when we fall.
Susan Sayers

94 Loving God,
because we trust you,
we come to you with our concerns.
When illness or injury
causes us disruption, uncertainty
and the prospect of long-term change;
when we find our lives spinning
out of our control;

give us working knowledge
of your total loving and unchanging presence,
so that in all the changes and troubles of life
we may be assured of your everlasting protection.

Susan Sayers

95 We pray that in all our relationships
you will make us effective channels
of your love and forgiveness.
Make us awash with your living water
so that our homes and places of work,
our shopping and leisure centres,
our conversations and actions,
are always in touch with the renewing power of God.

Susan Sayers

96 We stand alongside all those who are suffering,
whether in body, mind or spirit,
and long for your healing and comfort,
your strength for perseverance
and your patience in the dark times;
we long for your living Spirit to envelop and sustain them.

Susan Sayers

97 O God,
how we need you!
We thank you for supplying us and coaxing us forward
with such tenderness and affection. *Susan Sayers*

98 Holy God,
breathe your life into us;
breathe holiness and deepening faith,
breathe energy, inspired teaching and fervent praise;
unblock the channels and make us more receptive
to your gentleness and your power. *Susan Sayers*

99 Holy God,
breathe your life into us;
breathe responsible caring, honesty and compassion,
breathe right values and good stewardship,
peace and reconciliation, vision and hope. *Susan Sayers*

100 Holy God,
breathe your life into us;
breathe comfort and wholeness,
forgiveness and new confidence,
breathe peace of mind
and the knowledge of your love. *Susan Sayers*

101 Holy God,
breathe your life into us;
breathe courage for the journey
and the realisation that you can be trusted.
Breathe life that lasts for ever. *Susan Sayers*

102 Holy God,
breathe your life
into our homes and places of work;
breathe increased patience and understanding,
and the courage to live the Christian life
when to do so brings ridicule or demands sacrifice.
Susan Sayers

103 Holy God,
breathe your life into us now
as we offer you here our thanks and praise
for your life laid down out of love for us.
May our words be worked out
in fresh commitment to you.
Breathe into us,
that we may live in you. *Susan Sayers*

104 Heavenly Father,
increase our faith,
that we may be more ready
to trust you
and move forward with you
wherever you lead us. *Susan Sayers*

105 Heavenly Father,
grant us
the courage to be honest,
the will to be just,
the greatness to be humble
and the openness to learn. *Susan Sayers*

106 Heavenly Father,
at the door of our homes
place your welcome;
in the rooms of our homes, your love;
in the eyes of each of us, your truth;
and in all our companionship, your own.
You speak what is true,
and this truth will set us free. *Susan Sayers*

107 We give you thanks
for the loving example of Jesus,
who was obedient even to death
and strengthens us in all goodness. *Susan Sayers*

108 God of love,
be present in our hearts and homes,
to cherish, to challenge,
to reassure and to comfort us. *Susan Sayers*

109 Gracious God,
you are always
so much more ready to give than we are to receive;
open our hearts and minds
to live the costly way of love. *Susan Sayers*

110 Our heavenly Father,
you know us, your children,
so well and love us completely,
Father, knowing our weakness in the face of temptation,
we ask for your strength and protection
so that, though we stumble,
we shall not fall headlong.
Father, we are fighting temptation
and finding it difficult to resist.
We ask you to help us see clearly,
and equip us with all we need
to choose what is right. *Susan Sayers*

111 Father,
as we struggle to steer a straight course
true to your calling.
We pray for wisdom and courage,
honesty and the willingness to be vulnerable. *Susan Sayers*

112 Dear God,
we are confident
that you know and love each of us,
and understand our situation.
We pray for a deepening personal faith
and renewed faith whenever we are besieged by doubt.
Susan Sayers

113 Grant us the strength
to be vigilant and courageous
in upholding our Christian faith.
Make us also sensitive
to the language and culture
of each person seeking God
in their lives. *Susan Sayers*

114 We give you thanks and praise
for the endless love and patience you show us;
whenever we turn away,
please turn us back to you. *Susan Sayers*

115 Father,
we thirst for your meaning
and your guidance
in all our work and worship and praise.
Fill us so full with your Spirit
that those we meet are drawn to meet you. *Susan Sayers*

116 Father,
we thirst for your Spirit of love
which notices needs,
considers no job beneath itself,
and delights in each person's gifts. *Susan Sayers*

117 Loving God,
breathe your life into us,
so that we may speak your love to the world
and are willing to suffer
and prepared to sacrifice. *Susan Sayers*

118 Loving God,
breathe your patience and forgiveness
into our homes and all our relationships,
so that we learn to cherish and respect one another
and act with generosity. *Susan Sayers*

119 Loving God,
breathe your encouragement
into all our suffering and sadness,
so that the dark and painful times
become places of strong spiritual growth. *Susan Sayers*

120 Loving God,
breathe your grace
into our knowing and our feeling,
so that we rejoice each step of the way,
whatever the terrain.
You transform our lives through your love. *Susan Sayers*

121 Lord Jesus,
bring us all to life
by the power of your love.
Bring us all to live
in the life of your kingdom. *Susan Sayers*

122 Father,
if we are truly to be the body of Christ,
then let us stand at the foot of the cross
and learn what it means to love
and keep on loving;
to serve and keep on serving. *Susan Sayers*

123 Lead us into the desert of purging,
that through reflection and prayer
we may leave behind the things that tie our spirits down
and learn again to be your pilgrim people.
Through fasting from the frenzied feeding of false desires,
through study of your Word, meditation and acts of service,
restore the clearness of our seeing
and free us to share your generous love with all.
Ray Simpson

124 Help us to tread in the steps of Christ,
in the steps of Christ our Champion and King.
Show us the way when strong, when weak;
be our Guide in everything. *Ray Simpson*

125 O Holy Fire,
O Holy Grace,
O Overflowing Silent One:
by your birth
enable us;
by your overcoming of spirits
arm us;
by your integrity
make us true;
by your fortitude in trials
establish us;

by your self-giving in death
change us;
by your mission to unquiet spirits
raise us. *Ray Simpson*

126 Teach us to leave behind prejudice and meanness of spirit.
Incite us to generous giving.
Help us to create space for you
and play our part in the kingdom of your love. *Ray Simpson*

127 Humility of God,
who bowed your head upon the cross,
bend our necks low
that we may be led by you.
Arm of God,
you allowed your arms to be stretched out
on the wood of the cross.
Stretch out our arms in love of all through you.
Ray Simpson

128 Christ,
you are the refined molten metal
of our human forge.
Purge our desires,
strengthen our resolve,
sharpen our minds,
shape our wills. *Ray Simpson*

129 Christ of the scars,
into your hands we place the broken, the wounded,
the hungry and the homeless.
Christ of the scars,
into your hands we place
those who have been betrayed or bereaved;
those who have suffered loss of family or friends,
employment or home.
Christ of the scars,
into your hands we place neighbours defamed,
lovers spurned, spouses deserted.

Christ of the scars,
into your hands we place victims of war and crime.

Ray Simpson

130 Saving God,
by your incarnation and birth in poverty
set us free.
By your prayers and self-discipline
set us free.
By your tender works of mercy
set us free.
By your struggle for truth and justice
set us free.
By your nobility in persecution
set us free.
By your self-giving even in death
set us free.

Ray Simpson

131 *Prayer after Communion*
Bearer of pain and Maker of love,
steep our souls in yours,
that we may walk in your steps
through the pain to glory.

Ray Simpson

Mothering Sunday

132 Gracious God,
as a mother loves her child so you love us.
For that great truth
we praise and thank you.
We owe our very lives to you.
You have watched over us from our birth,
tenderly nurturing us,
showering us with love.
When we have needed you, you have been there.
You have given us strength in times of need,
comfort in times of distress,
encouragement in times of despair,
guidance in times of uncertainty.
Whatever we have faced, you have been with us.
Gracious God,
we have not always appreciated your love,
all too often ignoring what you would teach us,
disobeying your instructions,
taking you for granted and wandering far from your side.
Yet through it all your love has remained constant.
Gracious God,
caring for us more than you care for yourself,
sacrificing your all for our sakes,
loving us with an unquenchable love,
you have called us all to be your children.
For that great truth
we praise and thank you,
in the name of Christ. *Nick Fawcett*

133 Gracious God, 14/3/21
on this special day of thanksgiving
we catch a glimpse,
through a mother's love for her child,
of your love for us;
the care, dedication and devotion you show to all your children
which makes you as much 'our Mother' as 'our Father'.
For the intensity of your love,
Lord, we praise you.

As a mother nurtures her children,
instructing,
feeding,
clothing,
guiding,
so you nurture us,
carefully leading us towards maturity.
As a mother tends her children,
comforting in times of distress,
reassuring in times of uncertainty,
encouraging in times of challenge,
nursing in times of sickness,
so you tend us,
always there to lift us up
and set us on our feet again when we fall.
As a mother protects her children,
watching over them day by day,
alert to danger,
keeping them from harm,
and ready if necessary to sacrifice herself for their sakes,
so you protect us,
your arms constantly encircling us,
your hand delivering us from evil.
Gracious God,
Mother and Father of us all,
we rejoice today in the wonder of your love
and the constancy of your care.
Gratefully we respond,
in joyful worship
and heartfelt thanksgiving.
For the intensity of your love,
Lord, we praise you.
In the name of Christ, your only Son. *Nick Fawcett*

134 Forgive us, Lord,
for we take you for granted,
forgetting the way you hold us in your arms,
as a mother cradles her child;
the way you teach,
provide,

comfort and lead,
always there when we need you most.
Help us to respond,
not just today but every day,
in grateful and loving service. *Nick Fawcett*

135 Gracious God,
we are reminded today
of how easily we take a mother's love for granted,
failing to express our thanks for the care we receive,
slow to demonstrate our appreciation
for the patient nurture given over so many years.
We are reminded equally of how easily we take your love for granted,
failing to thank you for the blessings you shower upon us,
the care with which you daily surround us,
and the joy with which you fill our lives.
We have assumed that words do not need saying,
that our thankfulness can be taken as read.
We have believed love comes easily,
failing to recognise what it can sometimes cost.
We have imagined because no thanks is asked
that no thanks is necessary.
Gracious God,
help us to understand the joy we can bring
through saying thank you,
not just today but every day,
not just to our mothers but to everyone,
and not just to everyone but to you.
And help us, through the act of thanksgiving,
to recognise how much we have to be thankful for.
Nick Fawcett

136 Gracious God,
on this special day we thank you for mothers –
our own mothers and mothers everywhere.
We thank you for all they do, or once did,
all they give, or once gave,
all they mean, and will always mean.

Grant to all entrusted with the responsibility of
motherhood
your wisdom,
your guidance,
your support.
We thank you that you love us as a mother loves her child –
passionately, fiercely, devotedly, wholeheartedly –
and that, like a mother, you watch over us
every moment of every day,
seeking our welfare,
concerned about our progress,
equipping us for the journey of life.
You are always there when we need you,
ready to comfort, encourage and reassure,
slow to punish and swift to bless.
Gracious God,
we call you 'our Father',
but equally you are our Mother.
Help us to learn what that means,
and to rejoice in that truth. *Nick Fawcett*

137 Loving God,
we thank you for mothers –
for all they mean or have meant to us,
for the love they have shown,
and the care they have given.
We thank you for the dedication of mothers –
the sacrifices they make,
the support they offer,
the comfort they bring,
and the guidance they provide.
We thank you for the qualities of mothers –
their patience,
kindness,
concern
and understanding.
We thank you for the role of mothers,
the part they play in our lives,
our homes,

our society
and our world.
We thank you for the joy of mothers –
the pleasure,
enrichment,
laughter and fulfilment,
which raising children brings.
We thank you for time spent with mothers –
the learning,
playing,
caring and sharing,
which are part of family life.
Loving God,
we thank you for this day of saying thank you,
this opportunity to say what we so often mean to say
but so rarely do.
For mothers and motherhood,
for children and families,
we bring you this day our grateful praise. *Nick Fawcett*

138 Loving God,
we thank you for this day –
this day of remembering,
rejoicing,
and responding.
We thank you for our homes and all we associate with them –
the joy of family life,
the debt we owe to our parents,
and especially today the love of our mothers across the years.
We thank you for the much wider family of which we are
a part –
the family of humankind,
of this fellowship,
and the Church universal.
We thank you for the love you show us –
the same love a mother feels for her child,
the same patience and understanding,
the same concern and protectiveness.
Loving God,
grant your blessing upon all mothers and all families this day;

upon the family of humankind the world over,
upon the family of your Church, here and everywhere.
And grant your special care and support
to all those deprived of a mother's love,
and all those who have not yet come to know
your love for themselves.
Lord of all,
hear our prayer,
in the name of Christ. *Nick Fawcett*

139 Caring and compassionate God,
speak to us today through the love shown by mothers
of your love for us and all:
the love that brought us into being,
that has nurtured us across the years,
that welcomes us here
and that will go on reaching out,
come what may,
for all eternity.
Help us, as we honour what motherhood means,
to honour you also,
recognising that you show the same devotion and more,
an unswerving commitment to your children's welfare;
and teach us, as part of your family,
to respond accordingly,
loving you in return,
expressing our gratitude,
and living as you have taught us,
through Jesus Christ our Lord. *Nick Fawcett*

140 Gracious God,
you know what it is to love your children –
to watch over them tenderly, anxiously,
proudly, and constantly.
You know what this means,
for you have called us your children,
and you care for each of us
as deeply as a mother cares for her child.
So now we pray for those
entrusted with the responsibility of motherhood –

all those who watch over their children in the same way,
with the same feelings and intensity.
Grant to each one your wisdom, guidance, and strength.
We pray especially for single mothers –
those faced with the challenge
of raising a child or children on their own,
with no one else to share the demands or joys of parenthood.
Give to each of them patience, devotion, and dedication.
We pray for those who have lost their mothers
or have never known them,
those orphaned as children or given up for adoption,
those whose mothers have died;
all for whom this day brings pain rather than pleasure.
Grant them your comfort, your support,
and the assurance of your love always with them.
We pray finally for those who are separated from their children –
those whose children have moved far from home,
those who have suffered a miscarriage
or been through an abortion,
those who have endured the agony of a child's death.
Give to them your help, your solace, and hope for the future.
Gracious God,
you understand what mothers face,
what they give,
what they feel.
Accept our thanks for them this day,
and grant them your special blessing.
Lord of love,
hear our prayer,
in the name of Christ. *Nick Fawcett*

141 Gracious God,
on this Mothering Sunday we bring you our prayers
for all entrusted with the responsibility of motherhood.
We pray for mothers the world over,
recognising both the joys and demands they experience –
the privilege and pressures,
hopes and fears,
pleasure and pain that motherhood entails.

Equip them with the love, wisdom and strength they need.
We pray for single mothers,
bearing the responsibility of parenthood alone,
struggling sometimes to make ends meet,
and stigmatised by certain sections of society.
Grant them the emotional, physical and financial resources they need.
We pray for mothers who have experienced heartbreak –
their children stillborn or seriously disabled,
injured, maimed or killed through accident or assault,
struck down by debilitating disease or terminal illness.
Comfort them in their sorrow.
We pray for those denied the joy of motherhood –
enduring the trauma of infertility,
prevented on health grounds from risking a pregnancy,
or unable to establish a relationship
into which children can be born.
Help them to come to terms with their pain.
We pray for those who foster or adopt children,
those who long to do so but who are denied the opportunity,
and those who for various reasons
have given up their children
and who are haunted by the image of what might have been.
Grant them your strength and support.
We pray finally for those who long to discover their natural mothers,
those who have become estranged from them,
and those whose mothers have died –
all for whom Mothering Sunday brings pain rather than pleasure,
hurt rather than happiness.
May your love enfold them always.
Gracious God,
we pray for mothers and children everywhere.
May your blessing be upon them,
your hand guide them,
and your love enrich them all.

Nick Fawcett

142 Lord God,
we thank you for our earthly opportunities for
mothering and being mothered,
we also remember
the mothering of you,
our parent God. *Susan Sayers*

143 We pray to you, our loving parent God,
as children in one family.
We thank you, loving God,
for giving us one another to enjoy,
to laugh and cry with, to learn to live with.
May even our conflicts and arguments be used
in helping us to grow up in your love. *Susan Sayers*

144 Thank you, loving God,
for showing us the way to love
and giving us opportunities to give,
to take second place, to accept people as they are,
to forgive them when they annoy us,
and look for their needs before our own. *Susan Sayers*

145 Thank you, loving God,
for comfort and sympathy,
reassurance and practical caring when we are ill or sad.
Make us all more aware of the needs of those around us
and let our loving show in action. *Susan Sayers*

146 Thank you, loving God,
for your promise to be with us always,
and not just until we die.
We remember with affection
our parents who loved us into existence.
Gather us up into your loving arms
and comfort us even when our
memories remind us of loss and heartache. *Susan Sayers*

147 Thank you, loving God,
for giving us
space and support,
guidance and forgiveness,
challenge and reassurance. *Susan Sayers*

148 We gather together
in the presence of you, our parent God.
You provide comfort
in all our troubles and sufferings.
We are all your children:
help us grow in love. *Susan Sayers*

149 We thank you for the example of those
whose faith shines out through love in their lives.
Susan Sayers

150 Loving Father,
we give you thanks
for the comfort you provide
in all our troubles,
and for the richness
of all our relationships. *Susan Sayers*

151 Lord,
into our lives and relationships
pour the insight and discernment we need.
May we learn to love you more
as we learn to live and work in harmony,
focused on you and not on our divisions.
Pour the reality and wholesome truth we need,
that we may learn mutual trust
and support one another in love. *Susan Sayers*

152 Lord,
into the laughter and tears of family life
pour the freshness of your living presence,
as we work at our relationships
and deepen our love for one another. *Susan Sayers*

153 Lord,
may the way we live with one another
proclaim the truth of your constant love for us.

Susan Sayers

Palm Sunday

154 Blessed are you, Lord God of our salvation;
to you be praise and glory for ever.
As we rejoice this day
in the triumphant entry into Jerusalem,
may we too be willing to walk the way of the cross.
By our lives may we witness to you
as our Lord and King
and declare your saving love to the world. *David Adam*

155 Blessed are you, Lord God of all creation.
You have created us out of your love and for your love.
Help us to welcome you with songs of 'Hosanna',
knowing that you are our strength and our shield.
Help us to welcome Christ our Lord into our lives
as our Lord and Saviour. *David Adam*

156 Blessed are you, Lord Jesus,
for you are our Saviour.
As you were welcomed into Jerusalem,
may we welcome you into our homes and our lives.
Let our lives sing Hosannas to you,
that we may be full of your praise.
As we carry palm crosses
may we know the great sacrifice of love
that you made for us,
Jesus our Lord and King. *David Adam*

157 Blessed are you, Lord our God,
for you have redeemed us
by the offering of your Son upon the cross.
Through his death you destroy death
and open to us the kingdom of heaven.
As we seek to welcome Jesus into our lives
with cries of 'Hosanna',
and as we walk the way of the cross,
keep us ever mindful of your love and your peace.
David Adam

158 Lord God,
whose Son Jesus Christ
rode into Jerusalem as the Messiah,
to suffer and die,
bless these palms
that they may be to us a sign of his victory.
May we who hold them
always accept him as our King
until we rejoice in the kingdom
where he reigns with you and the Holy Spirit,
now and for ever. *David Adam*

159 Lord Jesus,
as you approached Jerusalem
the crowds welcomed you with loud 'Hosannas';
may we welcome you into our homes and our hearts
as our Saviour. *David Adam*

160 Lord God,
we hold these palm crosses as signs
of Jesus our King riding into Jerusalem as the Messiah
and of his suffering and dying on the cross.
Bless these palms that they may be to us
a sign of his victory and of your eternal love.
May we who hold them
always accept him as our King
until we rejoice in the kingdom
where he reigns with you and the Holy Spirit,
now and for ever. *David Adam*

161 Give us, Lord,
a sense of wonder in the presence of Christ,
an appreciation of the privilege we have,
day after day,
moment by moment,
of knowing the one who is not just sovereign
but the King of kings and Lord of lords,
greater than words can express or the mind comprehend.

Teach us to make time for him,
not as an extra or afterthought
but as our greatest joy and first priority,
offering him our grateful praise and thankful service.

Nick Fawcett

162 Lord Jesus Christ, 2017
you entered Jerusalem on a wave of enthusiasm,
greeted by your joyful people,
by shouts of praise and protestations of loyalty on every side.
Yet you knew that the bubble would soon burst,
that the welcome was only skin-deep.
We come today with equal gladness,
but conscious that our commitment,
like that of long ago,
may not be as strong as it should be;
our faith fickle if put to the test,
our loyalty flawed.
Speak to us through the story of that first Palm Sunday,
and through the events that followed,
and so may our hosannas ring out as loudly tomorrow
as they do today.
In your name we ask it.

Nick Fawcett

163 Saviour Christ,
King of kings and Lord of lords,
we want today to offer more than well-intentioned routine,
more than hymns and prayers,
words and music,
preaching and teaching.
We want to offer worship,
praise,
adoration,
bubbling up from within,
welling up,
spilling over,
expressing our love and gratitude,
and offering our lives back to you in joyful response.
Come among us now, through your Spirit,
and reveal your glory.

Fill and thrill us afresh with your grace,
and help us to bless your name,
as you have blessed us in so much. *Nick Fawcett*

164 Lord Jesus Christ,
we come to declare your greatness,
to acclaim you as King,
to profess our allegiance
and to seek your will for our lives.
Instruct us through this service,
so that, glimpsing the true meaning of power
and the nature of your rule,
we may commit ourselves more fully to you
and gain a clearer understanding of your purpose for all.
Nick Fawcett

165 Lord Jesus Christ,
we are good at singing your praises when life goes as we want it to,
but it's another matter when our expectations are overturned,
our preconceptions challenged and our faith tested.
We are eager to receive your blessings
but reluctant to take the way of sacrifice.
We are happy to proclaim you as king
but hesitant in offering our service.
So often our commitment is short-lived,
superficial and self-centred,
more about our own well-being than your kingdom.
Forgive us,
and, by your grace,
help us to offer you true allegiance,
whatever you may ask,
to the glory of your name. *Nick Fawcett*

166 Lord Jesus Christ,
we are reminded of how you entered Jerusalem
to shouts of joy and celebration.
But we remember too how quickly that welcome evaporated,
how soon the mood of the crowd changed.

Lord Jesus Christ,
we know all too well that we are not so different,
our commitment to you so often short-lived,
superficial,
self-centred.
Help us to welcome you into our lives with true gladness,
and to go on serving you come what may,
now and always. *Nick Fawcett*

167 Though we profess undying commitment, Lord,
too often we're like those who welcomed you into Jerusalem long ago,
swift to look the other way when commitment proves costly:
denying or abandoning you when service involves sacrifice.
Forgive the fragility of our faith,
and give us an allegiance that stays true
through thick or thin,
just as you stay true to us. *Nick Fawcett*

168 Lord Jesus Christ,
remind us through this day
that you are King, but not of this world;
that you rule, but not through force;
that you invite our respect, but do not demand it;
that you are the Lord of lords, but servant of all.
Give us a deeper understanding of your kingdom
and a firmer grasp of your will.
Teach us the way of humility and the path of love,
so that we may honour you now in worship
and each day in service,
to your glory. *Nick Fawcett*

169 Lord Jesus Christ,
we come today
remembering how crowds joyfully welcomed you
into Jerusalem,
but remembering also how a mob called there for your death,
the space of a few days making such a difference
to the response you received.

Help us, then, as we greet and acclaim you,
to search ourselves and examine the homage we offer,
so that the faith we profess today will be as real tomorrow
and every day
as it is now,
to the glory of your name. *Nick Fawcett*

170 Lord Jesus Christ,
you came to our world as the King of kings
and Lord of lords,
yet also as the servant of all.
You came deserving our praise and worship,
yet willingly accepting mockery, rejection and suffering
for our sakes.
You came to bring life in all its fullness,
yet you offered your life for the life of the world.
Lord Jesus Christ,
teach us to recognise the values of your kingdom
that turn our world upside down.
Help us to understand that strength lies in weakness,
greatness in humility,
and the secret of life in offering our lives to others.

Nick Fawcett

171 Loving God, 20/7
you call us to a journey of faith,
but sometimes that journey grinds to a halt.
We get stuck in a rut,
closed to new directions,
bogged down by the past,
or reluctant to step into an unfamiliar future,
preferring the view we know
to horizons that might stretch and challenge us.
Move within us through your Holy Spirit,
meet with us through the risen Christ,
and so give light to our path
that we may step forward in faith,
and travel onwards wherever you might lead,
through Jesus Christ our Lord. *Nick Fawcett*

172 Father,
as the crowds welcomed Jesus
and sang your praises,
we welcome you
into our hearts and lives
over the coming year.
We pray for opportunities
to spread your good news
and courage to take them. *Susan Sayers*

173 Father,
we recall the donkey Jesus rode on,
and we pray for that real humility in our hearts
which treats status and image casually,
and truth and loving service seriously. *Susan Sayers*

174 Father,
as the children sang and shouted your praise,
we pray for that same innocent trust in our lives
and the confidence to shout your praises
in our homes, our city and our land. *Susan Sayers*

175 Father,
the crowds were responding
to the healing love they had seen in action in Jesus.
We bring to you in our love and imaginations now
all the parts of our lives
which need your healing and help.
Give us comfort and reassurance,
wholeness and hope. *Susan Sayers*

176 Father,
we, too, spread our coats on the road
as we express our thankfulness
for all you have done for us
and the amazing extent of your love.
You are our God, we welcome you! *Susan Sayers*

177 Clip, clop, clip, clop!
Hosanna! Hosanna!
Hooray for Jesus,
the king on a donkey!
Hosanna! Hosanna!
Clip, clop, clip, clop! *Susan Sayers*

178 Noble Christ,
may we not become tortured souls
like those who tried to remove you from their puny
empires during your last weeks on Earth.
As we retread the last week of your earthly life,
may we so follow you in our hearts
that you will enter our hearts. *Ray Simpson*

179 O God,
when the ride is bumpy
and the world passes us by,
you pour out your life for us,
right to the very end.
When we are edged aside
and doors are shut in our face,
you pour out your life for us,
right to the very end.
When others are out to get us
and our home is not secure,
you pour out your life for us,
right to the very end.
When our lives are but a flicker
in the darkness that encroaches,
you pour out your life for us,
right to the very end. *Ray Simpson*

180 The One who created us
comes willingly to suffer for us;
let us spread our resolves before him
like branches of palm.

The Almighty comes to us
as one gentle and lowly of heart;
let us put on clothes of humility and praise.
The spirit is willing but the flesh is weak;
let us watch and wait with him. *Ray Simpson*

181 As your trial drew near, you looked upon
the city and wept over it, because it did not
recognise its salvation.
Open our eyes, that we may weep with you.
May we weep with you for the blindness of pride that
corrodes the dignity of human life . . .
Open our eyes, that we may weep with you.
We weep with you for the mad rush to consume
that tramples down on the Earth and its children . . .
Open our eyes, that we may weep with you.
We weep with you for the lust to control that
imprisons the soul and fragments community . . .
Open our eyes, that we may weep with you. *Ray Simpson*

Holy Week

182 Loving God,
through your Son you walked the way of the cross,
each step leading you inexorably to suffering, humiliation and death.
We know it,
and yet we continue to marvel,
for such love defies human logic,
transcending anything we can give in return.
Open our hearts afresh to the wonder of your love,
and help us to glimpse more fully all it cost you
and all it offers to us.
Help us to respond,
with grateful hearts
in joyful service,
to the glory of your name.

Nick Fawcett

183 Lord Jesus Christ,
you were under no illusions about those you called to follow you.
You knew that Judas would betray you,
Peter deny you,
and the rest of the Apostles forsake you,
yet still you continued on your way to the cross.
We marvel at your amazing grace that goes beyond our understanding.
Help us as we recall your suffering and death
to appreciate the wonder of your love for us,
and to love you in return.
In your name we ask it.

Nick Fawcett

184 Lord Jesus Christ,
we come today to remember,
to marvel,
to give thanks
and to worship.
We come to recall the agony you endured,
the sorrow, humiliation and despair,
and to celebrate the fact that you bore all this for people like us –
weak, foolish, faithless –

people who repeatedly fail you and betray your
awesome love.
Help us to glimpse today, through all we share,
more of what you have done for us,
to appreciate all that it cost you
and to respond with thankful, joyful hearts,
and lives consecrated to your service.
In your name we pray. *Nick Fawcett*

185 Lord Jesus Christ,
we remember today how you were betrayed,
abandoned,
denied,
your disciples' commitment evaporating
as the heat was turned on.
We come, conscious that our faith is likewise flawed and frail,
strong enough when little is asked of us
but vulnerable if put to the test.
Remind us, however, that you went to the cross
knowing our weakness,
ready to die for us despite our faults.
In that knowledge we come now –
humble,
thankful,
joyful.
Receive our praise. *Nick Fawcett*

186 Living Lord,
as we prepare again to celebrate your resurrection,
help us also to keep in mind what made it possible:
your readiness to endure the agony and anguish of the cross;
your love so great
that you were willing to lay down your life for our sake.
Write that truth once more in our hearts today,
so that the worship we offer now
will be reinforced by the love we show in turn,
to you,
to each other
and to all.
In your name we pray. *Nick Fawcett*

187 Too easily, Lord,
we follow the crowd –
the pressure to conform or desire to keep up
proving hard sometimes to resist.
Despite our best intentions,
we go astray, time after time.
Forgive us,
and teach us to follow not the sheep
but the shepherd. *Nick Fawcett*

188 We hear, Lord,
of how you were betrayed for thirty pieces of silver,
and we're shocked by the greed of Judas,
yet we're not as different as we like to think,
money shaping our lives in all kinds of ways.
Forgive our foolish ways,
for too often, without knowing it,
we sell out to the highest bidder,
and betray you in turn. *Nick Fawcett*

189 Lord Jesus Christ,
you didn't take the easy way as we would have done:
the path of popular acclaim,
of least resistance.
You took the right way:
the way of truth, love and service,
and you followed it faithfully,
knowingly,
undeterred by the consequences,
intent on serving others rather than yourself.
Forgive us that we are so easily led astray,
thoughts so much for ourselves and so little for you.
Forgive our willingness to compromise,
even when we know the way we ought to take.
Strengthen our resolve,
increase our faith,
and help us to stay true to our calling and true to you,
to the glory of your name. *Nick Fawcett*

190 Lord Jesus Christ,
you gave so much;
we give so little.
You refused to count the cost;
we resent even the smallest sacrifice being asked of us.
You took the way of others;
we take the way of self.
Lord Jesus,
all good, all loving,
we have no claim on your goodness,
no reason to expect your mercy,
yet, despite that, still you died for us.
Have mercy, we pray,
and, poor though it may be, accept the discipleship we offer,
and use us in the service of your kingdom,
to the glory of your name. *Nick Fawcett*

191 Lord Jesus Christ,
as we remember your triumphant entry into Jerusalem,
we are reminded of how easy it would have been
for you to take the easy option,
to follow the way of the world.
With the shouts of welcome still ringing in your ears,
the hosannas of the crowd still fresh in your memory,
it must have been so tempting to give them what they wanted,
to be the sort of Messiah they hoped you would be.
But with you there was no compromise,
no watering down of your message for the sake of popular acclaim.
You stayed true to your calling despite the inevitable consequences.
Lord,
we find it so hard to stay true in turn,
so difficult not to bend a little here
and give a little there.
Give us courage to walk the way of discipleship,
and, by your grace, to stay true to you
come what may.
In your name we pray. *Nick Fawcett*

192 Lord Jesus Christ,
we come again in this Holy Week
to reflect on your journey to the cross.
You knew where that journey was leading right from the very start,
and you did your best to ensure that your disciples understood too.
Yet they either couldn't or wouldn't believe
what you were telling them.
Forgive us that all too often we refuse to accept
what we don't want to hear.
Forgive us that we prefer to focus on the rewards of discipleship
rather than the cost.
Help us now, as we worship you,
to learn from your determination to complete the course
and, in turn, to run faithfully the race set before us,
looking to you,
the pioneer and perfecter of our faith,
in whose name we pray.

Nick Fawcett

193 Lord Jesus Christ,
as you cleansed the temple in Jerusalem,
overturning everything that defiled it,
that prevented it from fulfilling its true purpose
and that separated rather than united people with you,
so come now to our lives and cleanse our hearts,
removing in turn all that is unworthy,
that prevents us from being the people you would have us be,
that destroys our relationship with you.
Re-create us,
making our bodies into a living temple,
honouring to you and filled by your presence,
so that we may truly worship you now
and faithfully serve you always,
by your grace.

Nick Fawcett

194 Lord Jesus Christ,
you gave so much;
help us to give to you,
if only a little, in return. *Nick Fawcett*

195 Lord Jesus Christ,
you gave your all so that we might have life;
you counted yourself as nothing
so that we might rejoice in the wonder of your love;
you endured agony of body, mind and spirit,
so that we might receive mercy
and know the peace that only you can give.
Help us today to recognise more clearly everything you did for us,
and so inspire us to give something back to you.
Teach us to walk the way of the cross
and to bear the cost gladly for the joy set before us,
for your name's sake. *Nick Fawcett*

196 Lord Jesus Christ,
like those who stood at the foot of the cross,
watching as you writhed in agony,
as you cried out in despair
and as you breathed your last,
help us today to glimpse the astonishing extent of your love,
the immensity of your sacrifice
and the awful reality of what you suffered.
Help us to understand how much you love us
and how much you were ready to bear
to overcome everything that keeps us from you,
and may that knowledge feed our faith,
deepen our discipleship
and reinforce our resolve to follow you,
by your grace, and in your strength. *Nick Fawcett*

197 Lord Jesus Christ,
no matter how often we hear it,
how often we picture it,
we can barely begin to imagine what you went through on the cross.

We know you suffered,
we know you died,
but we cannot comprehend the agony you experienced,
or the terrible sense of isolation you must have endured
as the life ebbed from you.
We cannot imagine it,
but we need to try,
for only then can we recognise how much you loved us.
So we come today,
to listen again to words of Scripture,
to sing again well-loved hymns,
and to offer you our prayers,
our time,
our money
and our worship.
Receive all we bring,
and speak to us afresh of the immensity of your love
and the awesomeness of your grace,
for we ask it in your name. *Nick Fawcett*

Maundy Thursday

198 Lord Jesus Christ,
you broke bread with your disciples
you shared wine,
and you told them to go on doing likewise in memory of you.
For countless years,
across countless generations,
your people have done just that.
And so now we come,
to share in your supper,
and to remember.
This night of all nights reminds us of the great truths of the gospel –
of who you were,
what you did,
why you came,
and when you shall come again.
Help us, as we recall everything you went through in Gethsemane,
and all that went after,
to remember you did it for us as much as any.
To you be all praise and glory,
now and for evermore.

Nick Fawcett

199 Lord Jesus Christ,
you command us to eat and drink in remembrance of you,
and so we come now, recalling again the wonder of your love.
We remember how you shared bread and wine with your followers,
knowing that they would fail you.
We remember how in Gethsemane
you faced the awful and awesome prospect of the cross, alone.
We remember how you faced arrest, interrogation and brutality
with humility.
We remember your quiet acceptance of human hatred and evil
directed against you who knew no hatred and had done no evil.

We remember your willingness to embrace suffering
and death
so that we might find healing, wholeness and new life.
Lord Jesus Christ,
we remember your great love,
and we marvel at how much you were willing to bear for
our sakes.

Nick Fawcett

200 Lord Jesus Christ,
you broke bread, you shared wine –
with the one you knew would betray you,
with the one you knew would deny you,
with those you knew would soon abandon you to your fate.
Despite everything you stayed true,
freely offering your life.
Lord Jesus Christ,
you invite us to break bread and share wine,
even though we too betray you,
we too deny you,
we too abandon you time after time.
Despite everything, you stay true:
your body broken, your blood shed, for us!
Lord Jesus Christ,
we praise you and thank you with all our hearts.

Nick Fawcett

201 Lord Jesus Christ,
you spoke about loving our enemies,
praying for those who persecute us,
turning the other cheek,
and there in Gethsemane you showed that you meant
those words,
no matter what the cost.
Lord,
we are good at saying the right things,
but all too often it is merely talk,
found wanting when the real test comes.
Help us,
like you, to practise what we preach.

Nick Fawcett

202 Lord Jesus Christ,
your body was broken for us.
You endured the agony of the cross to reconcile us to God,
to break down the barriers that divide us,
to make us one.
Forgive us that we have erected new barriers in place of old,
barriers that divide us from one another,
that separate church from church
and Christian from Christian.
Help us to recognise that you died not just for some
but for all.
And help us to understand that nothing which keeps us apart
can be more important than the truth which binds
us together. *Nick Fawcett*

203 Lord Jesus Christ,
it's easy to condemn Judas –
the man who let you down,
the man who, with so much going for him, threw it all away.
Yet in our hearts we know we have no right to judge.
Each day in so many ways we betray you,
we betray ourselves, we betray our loved ones.
We say one thing but do another.
We talk of high ideals but we fail to reach them.
We mean well but we act foolishly.
Lord Jesus Christ,
save us from judging others, lest we too be judged.
Nick Fawcett

204 As we share this cup, Lord, we remember your words:
'My blood, poured out for you and for many,
for the forgiveness of sins.'
A cup not of pleasure but of pain,
drunk not for you but for all,
representing the greatest of gifts, precious beyond words.
Whenever we drink, Lord,
remind us of the true vine,
and the new wine you offer through it. *Nick Fawcett*

205 'If it is possible, take this cup from me.'
Lord Jesus,
we remember that desperate cry of yours
in the darkness of Gethsemane;
that cry of anguish as you faced up to the horror of the cross.
We remember that, knowing full well what the future held,
you were still able to say, 'Not my will, O God, but yours',
and you did so, not because you are different
but because you are fully one with us,
sharing our humanity,
ready, out of love, to offer your all
so that we might taste life in all its fullness.
Lord,
help us to recall everything you went through for our sakes,
and to appreciate the magnitude of what you did.
Teach us how much you loved us,
and so may we offer our love in return,
to you and to all,
for your name's sake. *Nick Fawcett*

206 Lord Jesus Christ,
we have broken bread,
we have shared wine –
and we have done it,
together with your people across the centuries,
in remembrance of you.
You promise that the time will come
when we share with you in your Father's kingdom,
a time when your will shall be done
and all things shall be made new.
Until then, may the memory of all you have done shape
our lives
and guide our footsteps,
to the glory of your name. *Nick Fawcett*

207 Lord Jesus Christ,
we hear so much as Christians about joy and celebration
that we can assume sometimes it is wrong to feel
anything else.

Yet in Gethsemane you knew the pain of sorrow;
the agony of betrayal, denial and rejection.
You experienced life at its darkest and found it hard to bear.
May that truth give us strength in times of need –
the ability to face grief openly and honestly,
knowing that you have been there before us
and that you understand all we are going through.

Nick Fawcett

208 Lord Jesus Christ,
we know the story of your death and resurrection so well
that we can forget sometimes what it actually involved,
overlooking the fact that you were human just as we are,
experiencing the same sorrow, uncertainty, pain and fear
that any of us would have experienced in your place.
You struggled there at Gethsemane with anguish of spirit
as you looked to the future,
striving to look beyond the cross but seeing only the agony of death,
yet you continued on your chosen path,
faithful to the last.
Lord Jesus Christ,
help us to realise the extent of your love,
and to offer at least a little of ours in return. *Nick Fawcett*

209 Lord Jesus Christ,
we remember today the hours of testing you endured
in Gethsemane:
the heartbreak you felt,
the fear you experienced,
the questions you wrestled with and the uncertainty
you faced.
We remember that, despite it all, you stood firm,
refusing to be swayed from your calling.
We remember how you went on to endure the agony of
the cross
and the darkness of death.
So now we come,
able to look forward in faith,

anticipating that time when we will share with you
in your Father's kingdom;
a time when there will be an end to sorrow and suffering,
sin and death.
Save us from ever losing sight of that destiny.
We look back,
we look forward,
and thus we commit ourselves in confidence
to your service here and now,
knowing that you are the same Lord,
yesterday, today and tomorrow –
the one in whom we can safely put our trust. *Nick Fawcett*

Good Friday

210 Help us today, Lord,
to recognise the awfulness of your death,
the awesomeness of your sacrifice;
to remember how nails pierced your hands and feet,
crushing flesh and bone,
the pain too dreadful to contemplate,
never mind the agony afterwards.
For the immense love that could endure all this,
willingly,
gladly,
for such as us,
receive our heartfelt praise. *Nick Fawcett*

211 Lord Jesus Christ, 2016
forgive us that, living as we do in the light of Easter,
we lose sight sometimes of the darkness of Good Friday.
Remind us today that for those who saw the life slip
from you
as you hung on the cross,
there could be no mistaking the truth,
no escaping the awfulness of the moment.
You endured the pain of betrayal,
the hurt of denial,
the humiliation of mockery
and, finally, the awful isolation of separation from your Father
as you took our sins on your shoulders –
and you did it for such as us.
Lord Jesus,
we marvel at your love;
at the fact that you were willing to go not just part of the way
but the whole way
to redeem the world.
We marvel that you,
in whom is life eternal,
were willing to experience death
so that we might taste that life.
Teach us today to appreciate the wonder of that sacrifice
and to recognise all that it continues to mean in so
many ways. *Nick Fawcett*

212 Lord Jesus Christ, 2016
we marvel again today at your astonishing love:
the way you endured the humiliation of Gethsemane,
the agony of the cross
and the darkness of the tomb,
not because you had to
but because you chose to.
We praise you that, despite the jeers and ridicule you faced,
your concern was always for others rather than yourself,
and thus you freely chose the way of humility, service
and self-sacrifice:
the lonely path of the cross.
Above all,
we praise you for your faithfulness to the last –
that though you could so easily have stepped down from
the cross,
you didn't;
and though you could have saved yourself,
you preferred instead to save the world.
Lord Jesus Christ,
however often we hear it,
still we are amazed by the magnitude of your love
and the awesomeness of your sacrifice.
Receive our praise and accept our worship,
for your name's sake. *Nick Fawcett*

213 Lord Jesus Christ,
whoever we are,
whatever we have done,
we know it is never too late to respond to your love,
for you are always ready to forgive and forget,
always waiting to pick up the pieces of our lives
and help us start again.
We praise you that this is why you came –
to offer a clean break to everyone who recognises their need;
a new beginning in this life and the life to come –
and, in that assurance, we come now seeking your help
and mercy,
for our sin and weakness is ever before us.

Lord Jesus Christ,
as the thief asked on the cross, so we ask too:
'When you come into your kingdom,
remember me.' *Nick Fawcett*

214 Speak afresh, Lord,
to us and your world,
of the cross of Christ and all it continues to mean;
of how he staggered under its weight
and hung on it finally in agony.
However familiar it may be,
save us from taking it for granted
and forgetting the awesome love of which it speaks.
Nick Fawcett

215 Remind us, Lord,
that your cross speaks not just of a single day,
but of every day,
changing every moment and everything.
Help us more fully to understand
and celebrate your grace,
so that it may shape our lives,
now, and always. *Nick Fawcett*

216 Living God,
in so many ways this is the blackest of days
recalling the darkest of moments:
a day on which hearts were broken
and faith tested to the limit,
a day of appalling suffering
and agonising death,
a day when all hell was let loose
and love seemed overwhelmed.
Yet we can call this day 'Good Friday',
for in all of that horror you were there.
In the despair,
pain,
humiliation
and sorrow,

you were supremely at work,
demonstrating the immensity of your love.
Living God,
as we recall those terrible yet wonderful events,
give us new insight into what you did that day,
for us and for all,
through Jesus Christ our Lord. *Nick Fawcett*

217 Lord Jesus Christ,
you suffered so much for our sakes –
pain of mind as well as body:
the pain of waiting for the end,
of mockery and rejection,
of betrayal, denial and misunderstanding,
of flogging and physical blows,
of thorns pressed on to your head
and nails driven into your hands and feet,
of hanging in agony on that cross.
Lord Jesus Christ,
as we celebrate all you have given us,
help us never to forget what it cost you. *Nick Fawcett*

218 Lord Jesus Christ,
broken for us,
remind us that the cross was not the end:
that from death came life,
from despair, hope
and from sorrow, joy –
your love bringing new beginnings.
And remind us,
above all,
that this same love is still at work,
here and now today,
able to take broken people,
broken lives,
and make them whole. *Nick Fawcett*

219 Lord Jesus Christ,
there are many who suffer,
many who endure untold agony of body, mind and spirit,

but few would do so willingly,
and fewer still choose that course as their vocation in life.
Yet you came and walked the way of the cross
with single-minded determination,
and you gave your life freely
so that one day there will be an end to all suffering
and sorrow;
a time when all will rejoice in the wonder of your love
and experience the joy of your kingdom.
Until then, Lord, reach out into our world of darkness,
into every place of need,
and bring the comfort, strength, peace and hope
that you alone can bring.
In your name we ask it. *Nick Fawcett*

220 Father,
if we as the Church
are truly to be the body of Christ,
then let us stand at the foot of the cross
and learn what it means to love and keep on loving;
to serve and keep on serving. *Susan Sayers*

221 If the world is ever to see real hope,
then purify and transform our lives
and stretch out our arms in loving forgiveness,
with no exceptions and no small print,
so that we shine as lights in the darkness. *Susan Sayers*

222 Father,
through the life-giving death of Jesus,
may we turn to you
and know your merciful love;
may we be comforted,
and may we all one day share
with those who have died
the eternal joy of your heaven. *Susan Sayers*

223 Father,
such amazing love is hard to grasp
and impossible to repay.
In thankfulness for lives set free to live
we offer you our selves. *Susan Sayers*

224 As we face up to the costly loving
shown by you, our God,
we approach you in humility
and pray to you now
to make us strong
to do your will in all things.
O God, in all the heartaches and joys
of human relationships,
may we be governed by selfless love,
faithful and forgiving like you,
without limit. *Susan Sayers*

225 You saw a widow give what she had;
help us to give our money with love.
You taught us to work like those who tend vines;
help us to tend the planet with love.
You taught that the poor are your family;
help us to serve the poor with love.
Through your defenceless love,
teach us the grace of self-offering.
Through your weakness,
teach us the grace of acceptance.
In your betrayal,
teach us the grace of forgiveness.
In your trials,
teach us the grace of trust. *Ray Simpson*

226 Lord Jesus,
you taught that your chosen people
can only fulfil their calling
if they become like a seed that dies,
buried in the earth, in order that many new ones may grow.
We pray that our brothers and sisters in Christ,
Palestinians and people of every race,

may know that they are now at the heart of your purposes
on Earth and in heaven.
Lord Jesus, as you are lifted up on a tree placed in the earth,
the rulers and empires of this world are exposed
for what they are – cheap and short-lived substitutes
for true government.
You become the way for true unity in the human family;
all who are buried, humbled and earthed
become your common ground.
So may it be. *Ray Simpson*

227 May we carry your cross
in our hearts through this day.
Your cross be in our eyes and in our looking.
Your cross be in our mouths and in our speaking.
Your cross be in our hands and in our working.
Your cross be in our minds and in our thinking.
Ray Simpson

228 You who lift the lowly and strengthen the frail,
who in your weakness raised a fallen world
and let sinners lift you on to a cross,
we thank you.
Lift each of us on to your shoulders
like a shepherd who does not neglect one lost sheep.
Lift us from Earth to heaven. *Ray Simpson*

229 Kind Father, faithful Saviour,
with head bowed your spirit passed across.
We thank you.
Receive us, at our end, into the hands of the Father.
Breathe your last for us and hold us up,
then raise us from the dead.
Cause the powers and principalities to fall back
that we may come swiftly to you. *Ray Simpson*
Echoes prayers on the Passion from the Anglo-Saxon Convent of Nunnaminster, Winchester, about AD 900, which combine Irish and Roman elements

230 Dearest Christ,
you have given love, given it exquisitely.
In your tiredness you washed your friends' tired feet.
In your generosity you gave bread to your betrayer.
In your all-seeing provision you bequeathed
a sacrament of bread and wine
that makes you constantly present to us.
In your anguish in the garden
you fought with demons and with doubt.
In your prayers you ever place your people
in the divine heart.
You call us to watch and pray.
Out of love for you we will watch and we will pray.

Ray Simpson

231 Crucified Christ, Son of the Father,
conceived by the Holy Spirit,
born of the Virgin Mary,
we adore you.
Crucified Christ, bearing contempt,
forgiving your enemies,
remaining always true,
we adore you.
Crucified Christ, treasure house of wisdom,
champion of justice, fount of love,
we adore you.
Crucified Christ, faithful to the end,
gatekeeper of paradise, eternal friend,
we adore you.

Ray Simpson

232 O King of the Friday,
whose limbs were stretched on the cross;
O Lord who did suffer
the bruises, the wounds, the loss;
we stretch ourselves beneath the shield of your might.
Some fruit from the tree of your passion
fall on us this night!

Ray Simpson

Echoes an early Irish prayer

233 Father,
look upon your family,
for whom our Lord Jesus Christ was willing to undergo
betrayal and torture.
Forgive our unfaithfulness.
Cure us of our sins.
Restore our unity.
Strengthen us to walk the way of the cross.
Bring us to the place of resurrection. *Ray Simpson*

234 The angel passed over the homes of the Godfollowers.
The fleeing people passed over the sea.
In their extremity you reached down to them, Lord.
Blessed be the God of eternal covenant.
The Christ walked the land doing works of mercy.
The tyrants dragged him to the gate of death.
In his extremity he called out to you
and you heard him.
Blessed be the God of eternal covenant.
O Christ, help us to become one with you.
In your weakness, teach us the grace of acceptance.
In your betrayal, teach us the grace of forgiveness.
In your trials, teach us the grace of trust.
In your defenceless love, teach us the grace of self-giving.

Ray Simpson

Saturday (Easter Eve)

235 We bless you for Mary
who with sorrow-pierced heart stayed with her son
at the foot of the cross.
We bless you for Joseph
who asked for the Life of all
to be laid in his garden of graves.
We bless you for the women
who adorned your grave with spices
and witnessed your resurrection. *Ray Simpson*

236 O Christ,
like the seed that falls into the ground
and yet bears fruit,
may we yet see the fruit of eternal life on Earth.
Ray Simpson

237 We thank you for Joseph,
who came to the governor by night
and asked for the Life of all to be laid
in his garden of graves.
We thank you for Mary, who with sorrow wept
as she saw her son hanging on the tree,
her heart pierced with sorrow.
We thank you for the women,
who went to the grave to watch,
to weep and offer fragrant spices of devotion.
We too will watch and weep and offer you
our tears,
our memories,
our tenderness,
our faith. *Ray Simpson*

238 Into our place of darkness,
into our place of strife,
into our fears and worries,
come with eternal life.
Into those who are dying,
into those weary of life,
into those lost and despairing,
come with eternal life. *Ray Simpson*

239 O Christ, you remembered those
who forgot your words about the sign of Jonah,
who after three days was delivered from the fish;
remember, too, those in our world who have lost hope.
O Christ, you remembered those
who went to their tombs without knowing you.
O Christ, go through the grave and the gates of death;
open to us the gate of glory. *Ray Simpson*

240 *For Easter Eve at the tomb/for devotion at the cross any time*

Lord, we offer you,
like the women who came to your tomb,
our tears, the memories of your life, the spices of our faith,
the ointment of our tenderness,
the flowers of our personality –
all, Lord, for you.
Lord, we offer you,
like the angels all gathered round your throne,
our songs of awe-struck devotion,
our shouts of your great victory,
our bowing low in reverence,
our joyful surrender of all we are –
all, Lord, for you.
Lord we offer you,
like your faithful disciples down the years,
our ears to listen to your every word,
our eyes to spot the needy ones,
our hands to touch with tenderness,
our hearts to embrace any hurting lives,
all, Lord, for you. *Ray Simpson*

Easter

241 Christ,
risen in glory,
scatter the darkness
from your heart and mind
and from the world,
that you may live in the fullness of life
and in awareness of his glorious kingdom.
And the blessing of God Almighty, the Father,
the Son and the Holy Spirit, be upon you now and for ever.

David Adam

242 Lord,
as we celebrate your resurrection,
strengthen your Church
to tell the Good News to the whole world.
Bless all who are called to teach and preach
in your name.
In the power of the risen Lord,
may they lead us from darkness
to his glorious light.

David Adam

243 With the whole Church
throughout the world and in heaven
we rejoice,
for Christ is risen.
Let every Christian rejoice,
let every heart rejoice,
for Christ is risen.

David Adam

244 Blessed are you, Lord our God.
On the first Easter Day
you raised your Son, Jesus Christ,
triumphant over death, sin and evil.
In his death you have destroyed death
and in his rising to life you have opened to us
the kingdom of heaven.
Blessed are you, Father, Son and Holy Spirit.

David Adam

245 May the Christ raised in glory
scatter the darkness from our hearts and minds
and from this world.
May the light of the risen Christ
shine upon us this day and always.
Alleluia, Christ is risen.
He is risen indeed.
Alleluia. *David Adam*

246 Blessed are you, mighty God,
Creator of light and darkness.
To you be praise and glory for ever.
By the resurrection of your Son to eternal life
you have destroyed the darkness and fear of death.
Radiant life is ours through him who loves us,
Jesus, our Lord and our friend.
Blessed are you, Father, Son and Holy Spirit,
our God for ever and ever. *David Adam*

247 Blessed are you,
God and Father of our Lord Jesus Christ.
To you be praise and glory for ever.
From the darkness of death
you have raised your Son to eternal life.
Through him death is destroyed,
light conquers darkness,
love defeats hatred
and your redeeming love is offered to us all.
Blessed are you, Lord God, for ever.
Alleluia. *David Adam*

248 God,
we thank you that seeds and bulbs grow in secret
without us seeing them.
We trust they will rise out of the earth.
We thank you for Jesus who,
though crucified, dead and buried,
rose again for us. *David Adam*

249 Blessed are you, Creator of life and joy.
We give you thanks for the promise of eternal life
offered through the death and resurrection
of your Son, Jesus Christ.
As we rejoice in the gift of this new day
we seek to delight in you and in your great love.
Blessed are you for ever. *David Adam*

250 Lord,
make us aware of your risen presence
in our lives.
May our worship be full of joy and awe.
Give us the courage to go out
to proclaim your love and your saving power. *David Adam*

251 Lord,
we are Easter people:
let 'Alleluia' be our song.
We give you thanks and praise
for the resurrection of our Lord Jesus Christ
and for his appearances to his loved ones.
We rejoice with the whole Church
in the joy of the risen Lord.
May we who know the Good News
go and tell others that he is risen. *David Adam*

252 Blessed are you, Lord our God,
for in your love you sent your Son Jesus Christ
to be our Saviour.
You deliver us from the darkness of sin and death
and open to us the way to eternal life.
Blessed are you, Father, Son and Holy Spirit.
To you be praise and glory for ever. *David Adam*

253 Glory and honour and blessing be yours,
great and mighty God.
In the resurrection you have destroyed death
and opened to us the gate of glory.
In you are life and life eternal.
We give you thanks and praise for ever and ever.

David Adam

254 Blessed are you, Lord God,
by whose power our Lord Jesus is raised from the dead.
In your presence is life and life eternal.
In your power death is conquered
and the gate to eternal life is opened.
In your presence is the fullness of joy. *David Adam*

255 Thank you, Lord,
that even in the darkest days of life
and the bleak chill of death,
you are there, bringing new beginnings.
For your life-giving power,
beyond containment,
receive our praise. *Nick Fawcett*

256 Whatever else we grow tired of, Lord,
help us still to celebrate the Good News of Christ –
something to go on getting excited about,
day after day. *Nick Fawcett*

257 Lord Jesus Christ,
for the victory you have won over sin and death,
and the victories you continue to win in our lives,
receive our praise. *Nick Fawcett*

258 Lord Jesus Christ,
you took on your shoulders
the crushing weight of human sinfulness –
and nailed it to a cross.
You endured the full force of human hatred –
and overcame it with love.
You entered the apparent finality of death –
and through it opened the way to life.
You took on the powers of evil –
and triumphed over them through good.
To you be praise and glory, now and for ever. *Nick Fawcett*

259 Gracious God, 2.16
we thank you that our faith is not founded on theory
or speculation –
on the ideas of theologians or the musings of philosophers.
It is rooted in what individuals have seen and heard,
in the living testimony of ordinary people like us,
in the witness of countless generations of believers
who have encountered the risen Christ for themselves
through his Spirit.
In him,
you came,
you lived,
you died,
you rose again,
making yourself known through the concrete events of
history.
For all who saw for themselves and passed the message on,
receive our thanks.
And for all that we experience today of your continuing love
and your life-giving purpose,
we give you our praise in joyful worship,
through Jesus Christ,
our risen, victorious Saviour. *Nick Fawcett*

260 Sovereign God, 2016
we don't understand how you raised Jesus from the dead –
how you breathed life into his broken body,
how you rolled the stone away from the tomb,
how he appeared unrecognised to Mary in the garden
and to disciples on the Emmaus Road;
how he walked through locked doors to be with the Apostles;
how he repeatedly appeared from nowhere
to stand among his followers.
What we do understand is this:
that he changed the lives of all who met him,
turning their sorrow into celebration,
their despair into hope
and their doubt into faith;
and that he is with us now through his life-giving Spirit,

remaking our lives in turn,
giving us joy, peace and a sense of purpose
such as we never imagined possible before.
We do not understand, but we believe,
we rejoice
and we offer you our grateful worship
in the name of that same Jesus,
our risen Lord and Saviour. *Nick Fawcett*

261 Living God,
we praise you for the great truth of Easter –
the message that your love will not be defeated.
When human evil had done its worst,
despite every effort to frustrate your purpose,
still your will triumphed!
The stone was rolled away,
the tomb was empty,
Christ had risen!
May that truth fire us each day with new hope,
new confidence,
and new enthusiasm,
knowing that whatever obstacles we may face
and whatever may fight against us,
there is nothing that will finally be able to thwart
your purpose
or to deny your saving purpose,
in Jesus Christ our Lord. *Nick Fawcett*

262 Lord Jesus Christ,
we praise you that we can worship you
not simply as the crucified Christ
but as our risen Lord and Saviour.
We praise you that death was not the end but a
new beginning,
not simply for you but for us!
We praise you for this time of joy, thanksgiving and
rejoicing,
a time that speaks of victory, renewal and hope.

For the great message of Easter
that has spoken to countless people across the years
and that continues to speak to us today,
receive our joyful and grateful worship.
Come among us now, in your risen power,
and send us out to proclaim your name
and live to your glory,
for your name's sake. *Nick Fawcett*

263 Lord Jesus Christ,
you appeared to different people
at different places
at different times:
to Mary in the garden,
to Cleopas and his companion on the Emmaus Road,
to the disciples in the upper room,
to your followers in Galilee.
Each had their own unique encounter with you,
and it was only when you met with them,
face to face,
that the truth dawned;
only then that they dared to believe you were alive.
Lord Jesus Christ,
we cannot see you quite as they did,
but we too can meet with you
and experience the reality of your living presence.
Meet with us now, as we worship you.
Live in us always
so that our lives might resound to your praise and glory.
Nick Fawcett

264 Living God,
we praise you for the wonder of Easter –
this day that changed the world for ever!
We rejoice in the victory of Christ:
his triumph over evil,
hatred,
despair,
and even death itself.

Living God,
we praise you for the victory you have won,
and for the assurance it brings that nothing in life or death
can ever separate us from your love;
nothing in heaven or earth defeat your loving purpose for
all the world.
To you be praise and glory,
this day and always. *Nick Fawcett*

265 Living God,
we praise you once more for the good news of Easter,
the triumphant message of resurrection –
new hope,
new joy,
new life!
We praise you for the truth at its heart:
that your love could not be kept down,
your purpose could not be defeated
and your mercy could not be destroyed.
Teach us that what was true then is true now –
that nothing can stand in the way
of your sovereign power and redeeming grace.
Assure us, then,
even when faith seems to fly in the face of reason,
to trust in you,
confident that your will shall be done
and your kingdom come,
through Jesus Christ our Lord. *Nick Fawcett*

266 Sovereign God,
sometimes it seems too good to be true –
the cross,
the empty tomb
and the promise of new life for all eternity.
There are times when,
for all our faith,
we struggle to accept it,
not because we don't want to
but because we want to so much,

and we wonder whether we are fooling ourselves,
telling ourselves what we want to believe.
Yet you remind us today that this is precisely how the Apostles felt
until they met with the risen Christ
and knew the truth for themselves,
not as speculation
but as an indisputable experience.
Rekindle our faith this Easter time.
Assure us,
through experiencing again
the presence of the risen Christ within our hearts,
that with you nothing is too good to be true,
for you are able to do more than we can ask or imagine.
To you be praise and glory,
now and for evermore. *Nick Fawcett*

267 Sovereign God,
we praise you today for the power of the gospel;
the way across the centuries it has spoken to so many lives.
We praise you for everything you achieved in Christ,
transforming not just individuals but the very course of history
through his life, death and resurrection.
We praise you that you involved yourself in human history,
not standing aloof from our need
but sharing our humanity so that we might share your eternity.
For your life-giving grace that continues to reach out into the world
and for your mighty strength that will never rest
until your will is done and your kingdom come,
receive our glad and joyful worship,
in the name of Christ. *Nick Fawcett*

268 Sovereign God,
rejoicing in the glorious fulfilment of your promises,
your living, dying and rising among us through your Son,
we bring you now our praise, thanksgiving,
worship and commitment.

Open our lives afresh to your word
and to the presence of the risen Christ.
Thrill us as we celebrate your faithfulness and sovereignty –
the great victory of your love –
and so may we go on our way today,
your word on our lips,
your joy in our eyes
and your love in our hearts,
through Jesus Christ our Lord. *Nick Fawcett*

269 Lord Jesus Christ,
as Mary recognised you in the garden,
as disciples met you on the Emmaus Road,
as the Apostles encountered you standing among them
and as Thomas knelt before you in homage,
his doubts and questions overcome,
so we would meet you now,
our risen Lord and Saviour,
conqueror of evil,
triumphant over death.
We would acknowledge your greatness,
acclaim your love,
salute your victory
and celebrate the new life you have given –
the hope, joy, peace and blessing
you have poured into our hearts.
Accept, then, our worship,
and meet us through it. *Nick Fawcett*

270 Risen Saviour,
though we have not seen the empty tomb and folded grave-clothes,
the wounds in your hands and feet,
or your physical presence among us,
yet we believe,
for we have tasted your love,
experienced your power,
known you deep within us through your Holy Spirit
bringing joy, peace and fullness of life.

So we come today, simply to acclaim you,
to bring our worship,
to express our gratitude,
to acknowledge you in praise, wonder and adoration,
as our Lord and our God. *Nick Fawcett*

271 Lord Jesus Christ,
we celebrate again today your triumph over falsehood and evil;
the fact that all the attempts to discredit you
and to suppress the truth of your resurrection
came to nothing,
for it was impossible to deny the reality of your presence
in the hearts of those who knew you.
Forgive us that we are not always as truthful as we should be,
slipping so easily into white lies,
or hiding behind half-truths.
Remind us that your truth can set us free,
and so teach us to receive it with joy,
speak it in love and live by it in faith,
trusting in your love that alone will never fail.
In your name we ask it. *Nick Fawcett*

272 Thank you, Lord,
that you do not leave us alone,
instead drawing alongside us each day.
Thank you that,
just as you met with your followers on the road
and your disciples in the upper room,
so, in Christ, you meet with us in the journey of life,
always there, in your resurrection power,
to guide, protect, comfort and support,
each of us valued as a little child,
chosen and precious to you. *Nick Fawcett*

273 Lord Jesus Christ,
we thank you for the great message of Easter –
that in what the world counted defeat you won the greatest of victories.

We praise you for your triumph over evil and death,
and for everything this has meant over the years to so many people.
Most of all,
we thank you for our own experiences of your resurrection power –
the times you have brought us victory
over all that stops us living life to the full.
Teach us to live each day in the light of what you have done,
confident that no situation,
however dreadful it may seem,
is finally beyond your power to redeem,
and so may we put our trust in you always,
for this life
and the life to come. *Nick Fawcett*

274 Great and wonderful God,
today of all days we would praise you.
We would bring you our worship,
our gratitude,
our faith
and our lives,
offering them to you in joyful celebration
at the victory you have won for us in Christ.
Grant, then, that everything we offer you today
will speak of our joy, devotion
and desire to follow Christ;
to give ourselves to him as he gave himself for us.
Nick Fawcett

275 Sovereign God,
we thank you that Easter is not just about events long ago
but about now;
not just about others
but about us;
not just about certain aspects of life
but about life itself!
We thank you for the truths of Easter we can continue to celebrate today:

the victory of good over evil,
love over hate,
and life over death;
the turning of weakness into strength,
fear into courage,
and doubt into faith;
a new beginning where it had seemed like the end,
hope where there had been despair;
and confidence where there had been confusion.
Help us to live each day in the light of Easter,
with its joy bubbling up in our hearts,
its laughter shining from our eyes,
and its message always on our lips.
So may others,
seeing the difference it has made to us,
discover the difference it can make for them,
through Jesus Christ our Lord. *Nick Fawcett*

276 Living God,
your ways are not our ways,
neither are your thoughts our thoughts.
There is so much in our lives that troubles and confuses us,
so much hurt and pain that we cannot begin to make sense of.
Yet we know that in Jesus you have shared our humanity,
experiencing not just the good but the bad.
You understand what it means to be hurt,
to endure suffering,
to face even death itself.
As well as our joys you have shared our sorrows.
Living God,
we thank you for the assurance this gives us:
that whatever we face you will be with us in it.
Teach us to approach each day in the light of that truth,
and so to live always as your Easter people,
to the glory of your name. *Nick Fawcett*

277 Lord Jesus Christ,
we thank you that you meet us day by day,
just as you met your disciples in the days following your resurrection.
We thank you that your victory of good over evil,
love over hate
and life over death
continues to make such a difference to our lives,
just as it did to theirs,
bringing new beginnings when it seems like the end,
new hope where there seems only despair.
For turning weakness into strength,
fear into confidence
and doubt into faith,
receive our praise
and continue to work that miracle in our lives and our world today,
making all things new,
to the glory of your name. *Nick Fawcett*

278 May the wonder of this season, Lord,
point to a deeper wonder:
your resurrection power that makes each day springtime,
each moment a new dawn, full of promise.
Help us to recognise that with you,
every apparent ending leads to a fresh start,
death itself the gate to life. *Nick Fawcett*

279 Risen Lord,
remind us of the way you changed the lives of the apostles
and of countless others since,
transforming doubt to faith,
sorrow to joy
and fear to confidence.
Meet us, then, through the risen Christ,
so that, incredible though it may seem,
we may know him for ourselves,
and share his life,
now and for evermore. *Nick Fawcett*

280 Living God,
speak today and every day of the empty tomb
and your risen Son –
of your resurrection power bringing new birth,
new life.
Help us to greet this season with childlike enthusiasm,
eager to celebrate your resurrection power and renewing love –
what this season is really all about:
the Good News at its heart. *Nick Fawcett*

281 Speak, Lord,
of your resurrection power
through which your Son rose again
and his followers bounced back from despair.
Grant the assurance that,
however low life may bring us
and however hard we may fall,
you will lift us up to new horizons,
both now and for all eternity. *Nick Fawcett*

282 Teach us, Lord,
that though truth may be threatened by falsehood,
good by evil,
love by hatred
and life by death,
your purpose will always come through,
nothing finally being allowed to frustrate your
renewing power
and redeeming grace. *Nick Fawcett*

283 Save us, Lord,
from sentimentalising this season,
settling for cosy pictures of daffodils and Easter bunnies,
and forgetting what it cost you to bring us life.
Remind us of how much you gave that we might receive,
and help us to give something back in return,
offering our love, our life,
our all to you. *Nick Fawcett*

284 Help us to remember, Lord,
that Easter is not a holiday but a holy day,
speaking of you and your love in Christ,
his resurrection and the life you promise us in turn.
Wherever we are, then, and whatever we do,
help us to remember what this season is ultimately about,
and to make space for you as well as for us. *Nick Fawcett*

285 Remind us, Lord,
when shadows darken our lives,
and light seems suddenly extinguished,
that you entered the darkness of death and rose victorious;
that you experienced the full force of hatred
and conquered it with love;
that you took on the powers of evil
and worked through them for good.
Remind us, then,
that your light will always shine,
nothing in heaven or earth finally able to overcome it.

Nick Fawcett

286 Lord Jesus Christ,
come to us afresh each day
and teach us to meet and greet you
so that we may know you as a friend and companion,
serve you as Saviour
and confess you as the risen Lord,
to the glory of your name. *Nick Fawcett*

287 Lord of all,
despite everything that conspires against it,
help us to hold on to the conviction
that good will finally conquer evil,
and your love triumph over all. *Nick Fawcett*

288 Teach us, Lord,
that you are constantly at work,
striving against everything that frustrates your will
and denies your love.

Teach us to hold on to those moments in life
when wrongs are righted and justice is done at last.
Above all,
teach us to look at the cross of Christ,
and to draw strength from the victory of love
over what had seemed to be the triumph of evil.

Nick Fawcett

289 Lord Jesus Christ,
you faced up to evil,
even though it cost you your life to conquer it:
give us wisdom to know when we must stand up for
our principles,
and then courage to stand firm,
for your name's sake. *Nick Fawcett*

290 Sovereign God,
teach us that,
even where evil has done its worst,
where darkness seems victorious
and where hopelessness seems unrelieved,
you are still there,
working in all things for good,
nothing able finally to frustrate your gracious purpose
in Jesus Christ our Lord. *Nick Fawcett*

291 Living God,
teach us that the gospel not only sounds like good news;
it is good news! *Nick Fawcett*

292 Lord Jesus Christ,
as you rose victorious over death,
so may hope, faith and love
continue to triumph in our lives
over everything that conspires against them. *Nick Fawcett*

293 Lord Jesus Christ,
may the message of your glorious resurrection
continue to stir our hearts and change our lives today,
just as it has spoken to so many across the years.

Nick Fawcett

294 Lord Jesus Christ,
like the two disciples on the Emmaus Road,
so often we journey through life unaware of your presence.
Though we talk of your resurrection
it does not stir our hearts or capture our imagination
in the way it should.
Yet even though we may not realise it,
you are there with us,
matching your stride to ours,
waiting to meet us along the way.
Open our eyes
that we may see and know you better. *Nick Fawcett*

295 Lord Jesus Christ,
we rejoice today in the good news of your resurrection.
You met with Mary in the garden,
bringing laughter after tears.
You met with women returning from the tomb,
bringing confidence after confusion.
You met with Cleopas on the Emmaus Road,
bringing hope after dismay.
You met with the Apostles in a room barred against
the world,
bringing joy after sorrow.
You met with Thomas, in his disbelief,
bringing faith after doubt.
You met with Paul on his way to Damascus,
bringing love after hatred.
You met with countless generations across the centuries,
bringing renewal after rejection.
Meet with us now, in this day, this moment,
bringing light after darkness.
Fill our hearts with the new life of Easter,
until that day when, with all your people,
we enter your kingdom
and rejoice in the wonder of your love for all eternity.
In your name we pray. *Nick Fawcett*

296 Lord Jesus Christ,
you brought new beginnings out of what had seemed the end;
new hope in what had seemed hopeless;
new purpose in what had seemed to deny all meaning.
We celebrate that truth,
yet we confess how hard we find it sometimes
to believe that such new beginnings can apply to us;
that we too can start again.
We look at our own situation –
the opportunities missed,
hopes dashed,
possibilities denied,
and dreams extinguished –
and we see no prospect of life rising fresh from the ashes.
Yet, as you came to Mary, the Apostles and countless others since,
so you come now afresh today
in your life-giving, renewing power.
Teach us,
however hopeless circumstances might seem,
however much we may feel ourselves to be at a dead end,
never to lose our sense of all that you are able to do.
Remind us that endings can lead to beginnings,
that new life can spring from old,
and so may we look forward with confidence
to everything you will yet do in our lives.
In your name we ask it. *Nick Fawcett*

297 Risen Lord,
as we meet and greet you in worship,
cause our spirits to leap and hearts to dance within us
at the good news of your resurrection:
the triumph of love,
the victory of good,
the conquest of death by life.
Enthral us again with that glorious message of the gospel,
so that we will go on our way rejoicing,
proclaiming the new life you have won for all,
and making disciples in your name. *Nick Fawcett*

298 Lord Jesus Christ,
as those who walked with you on the Emmaus Road
recognised you in the breaking of bread,
so may we recognise you now as we join in worship.
Grant that we too may meet with you,
walk with you
and talk with you,
so that our hearts might burn within us
as we go on our way, rejoicing.
Open our hearts, today and every day,
to your living presence and life-giving power. *Nick Fawcett*

299 Transforming God,
turning sorrow to joy,
doubt to faith,
despair to hope,
and death to life,
put your hand upon us,
and through this time set apart for you
continue to make us new.
Turn our weakness into strength,
our pride into humility,
our anxiety into trust,
and our faithlessness into obedience.
Take what we are,
and, by your resurrection power,
shape what we shall be,
through Jesus Christ our Lord. *Nick Fawcett*

300 Lord Jesus Christ,
you came to bring us life in all its fullness;
to offer hope beyond the grave.
Teach us that death is not the end, but a new beginning –
the gateway to life everlasting.
And may that confidence shape our attitude not only
towards death
but towards life also.
May we live each day in the context not just of the here
and now

but of eternity,
knowing there is nothing in heaven or earth
that shall ever finally be able to separate us from your love.
Nick Fawcett

301 Remind us, Lord,
that Jesus died,
not just playing a part
or going through the motions,
but enduring the darkness of death itself.
Yet remind us also that he rose again,
greeting his disciples in the upper room,
meeting them on the road,
restoring faith, hope, joy and purpose.
So then, to all facing the agony of bereavement,
the trauma and despair of loss,
give the assurance that beyond the grave lie new beginnings;
that from dust and ashes you will bring new life,
now and always. *Nick Fawcett*

302 Lord Jesus Christ,
it was not just you who was broken on a cross –
it was your disciples too,
their hearts broken just as surely,
their dreams and hopes snuffed out,
their faith cut from beneath them and laid to rest.
It was not just you who rose again –
it was your disciples too,
their hearts beating once more with joyful anticipation,
their vision for the future reborn,
their faith rekindled, bursting into unquenchable flame.
Come to us now where we are broken –
where love has died,
hope has faded,
faith grown cold.
Reach out and touch us in body, mind and spirit,
and help us to walk in the newness of life
which you alone can bring.
In your name we ask it. *Nick Fawcett*

303 Living God,
we look at the world and at our lives
and we are dismayed sometimes at how little seems to change.
We go on making the same mistakes we've always made,
and all around us there seems to be as much sorrow,
suffering,
hatred and evil as there has ever been.
Help us to hold on to the conviction that life can change;
to remember how,
in the resurrection of Christ,
you overcame the power of sin and death.
Help us to remember that
though everything may seem to conspire against you,
you have won the victory through him –
a victory that nothing can ever undo –
and so may we trust in your ability to transform and renew
all things,
by his grace. *Nick Fawcett*

304 Renewing and life-giving God,
as we celebrate again your victory over death
and your triumph over evil,
open our hearts today to the way you are able to change
our lives
and transform our world.
Remind us of your resurrection power all around us,
bringing hope out of despair,
joy out of sorrow,
peace out of turmoil
and love out of hatred,
and in that faith may we live now and trust for the future,
assured that nothing can defeat your purpose
or deny the life you offer for all eternity,
through Jesus Christ our Lord. *Nick Fawcett*

305 Lord Jesus Christ,
meet with us now through your Spirit.
In a world where so much questions faith,
denies love

and threatens hope,
may your resurrection life flow within us,
convincing us of your eternal purpose:
the blessings you hold in store –
imperishable,
unfading,
kept in heaven –
and may that assurance sustain us now and always.

Nick Fawcett

306 As we celebrate
the new life of Resurrection,
we pray to you,
the one true God,
who brings us all to life. *Susan Sayers*

307 Lord God,
may we proclaim with joy
your message of hope
for the world;
may our lives,
as well as our worship,
testify to the truth
of the Resurrection;
broaden our vision
of what is possible
through new life in you. *Susan Sayers*

308 Life-giving God,
you transform our lives.
We thank you for our lives well lived,
through the resurrection hope,
may we know the joy of heaven. *Susan Sayers*

309 Lord God,
we thank you for the precious gift of new life;
may we never again take it for granted,
but live each moment in the fullness of life
that Jesus has gained for us. *Susan Sayers*

310 We bring to you, Lord,
our lives in all richness and need;
all diversity and division.
Give us a fresh understanding
of what it means to live in you;
may all of us celebrate
the reality of your presence among us,
filling us with new life and new hope. *Susan Sayers*

311 Walk with us, Lord,
on our journey of faith,
both as individuals and as the Church of God;
open up to us the truths you long for us to understand,
and inspire all who teach and encourage.
Equip us all to pass on the good news of Easter.
Susan Sayers

312 Lord of life,
may we be alive with your risen life,
refreshed and revived by the breath of your Spirit,
purified and refined like gold and silver,
so that we truly offer the possibility
of saving love to the searching world. *Susan Sayers*

313 As we celebrate the risen Christ,
we pray to you, the God of life,
in whom we live. *Susan Sayers*

314 We thank you with gratitude
for your presence
all over the world.
We rejoice today
in the wonder of the Resurrection. *Susan Sayers*

315 We give you thanks and praise
for the salvation and restoration
that is now possible for us
through Christ's victory over death. *Susan Sayers*

316 Jesus,
who stopped the wind and stilled the waves,
grant you calm in the storm times.
Jesus, victor over death and destruction,
bring safety on your voyage.
Jesus of the purest love, perfect companion,
bring guarding ones around you.
Jesus of the miraculous catching of fish
and the perfect lakeside meal,
guide you finally ashore. *Ray Simpson*

From 'The First Voyage of the Coracle',
Community of Aidan and Hilda

317 Risen Christ,
you burst from the grave;
help us to burst into life.
You breathed on your disciples;
breathe your life into us. *Ray Simpson*

318 In our baptism, O Lord Christ,
our self-centred life is buried
and we rise up with your new life in us.
Day by day may we be buried;
day by day may we rise with you. *Ray Simpson*

319 Risen Lord,
you revealed yourself
to Mary in the garden at dawn.
Reveal yourself to us in the dawnings of our lives.
Risen Lord, you revealed yourself
to the fisherfolk as they toiled in vain at their work.
Reveal yourself to us in the long hours of our toil.
Risen Lord, you revealed yourself
to the walkers as they welcomed you into their home.
Reveal yourself to us as we walk
and make welcome our homes.
Risen Lord, you revealed yourself
to Thomas when he felt the scars in your body.

Reveal yourself to us
as we reach out to the scars of the world.
Risen Lord, you revealed yourself
to many as they met beneath the skies.
Reveal yourself to us in the wonder of your creation.

Ray Simpson

320 Christ Jesus,
in the light of your risen presence
and in union with your first frail apostles, we say sorry:
for not weighing your words,
for not sharing your trials,
for not believing your promises. *Ray Simpson*

321 Risen Christ,
you turned Mary's tears into joy;
turn our tears into joy.
Risen Christ, you turned the travellers' despair into hope;
turn our despair into hope.
Risen Christ, you turned the disciples' fears into boldness;
turn our fears into boldness.
Risen Christ, you turned an empty catch into fullness;
turn our empty routines into fullness.
Risen Christ, you turned Thomas' unbelief into trust;
turn our unbelief into trust. *Ray Simpson*

322 May Christ rise in glory,
scattering the darkness before your path.
The Sun of suns,
the eye of the great God,
the eye of the King of hosts,
is rising upon us,
gently and generously.
Welcome, glorious Son,
dawn of a new day. *Ray Simpson*

323 Through the resurrection of your Son you overcame
the hold of sin and death.
Transform us in all our ways. *Ray Simpson*

Easter Eucharist

324 Risen Christ,
you called Peter to love you and feed your flock.
We, too, accept your call to love you
and nourish those who hunger for you.
Risen Christ,
you burst from the grave.
Now burst into life through us. *Ray Simpson*

325 Risen Christ,
as you appeared to your disciples
in the breaking of bread,
come to us afresh in this Eucharist.
You call us to be open to the coming of your Spirit.
Give us receptive, waiting and eager hearts
to receive all that you wish to give us. *Ray Simpson*